THE EPISTLE TO THE HEBREWS
and
THE EPISTLE OF ST. JAMES

NEW TESTAMENT FOR SPIRITUAL READING

VOLUME 21

Edited by

John L. McKenzie, S.J.

THE EPISTLE
TO THE HEBREWS

F. J. SCHIERSE

THE EPISTLE
OF ST. JAMES

OTTO KNOCH

CROSSROAD · NEW YORK

1981
The Crossroad Publishing Company
575 Lexington Avenue, New York, NY 10022

Originally published as *Der Brief an die Hebräer*
and *Der Brief des Apostels Jakobus*
© 1964, 1968 by Patmos-Verlag
from the series *Geistliche Schriftlesung*
edited by Wolfgang Trilling
with Karl Hermann Schelke and Heinz Schürmann

English translation © 1969 by Burns & Oates, Limited, London
Translated by Benen Fahy

Library of Congress Catalog Card Number: 81-68179
ISBN: 0-8245-0130-6

PREFACE

The epistle of James is the first in that portion of the New Testament which is called the Catholic or General Epistles. This group is so designated because, with the exception of 2-3, the epistles are not addressed to any particular church or person, as the letters of Paul are. In character the epistle to the Hebrews is also Catholic or General; it has no address, and its contents do not suggest that it is addressed to Jewish Christians, the only possible meaning of Hebrews. The title does not belong to the epistle, and it is not known how this unsuitable title became attached to the document. 12:22-25 contain a conclusion in epistolary form; but these verses follow the doxology of 20-21 and are almost certainly secondary. Hebrews very probably is not originally an epistle or a letter, and originally it had no title, or no title which has survived.

The epistle of James, on the other hand, was written by a Jewish Christian for Jewish Christians. The content makes this reasonably certain, and if any New Testament document should be called an epistle to the Hebrews it is the epistle of James. This does not, however, imply that it has no message for modern readers; and the reader is referred to the introduction and commentary for an exposition of the lasting significance of the epistle.

The introductions show the reader that these two epistles have each their own character, notably different from the epistles of Paul. With a few exceptions, the epistles of Paul were written in response to particular problems of particular churches. Hebrews and James are addressed to no one in particular; they are tracts rather than epistles. It is impossible to articulate the problem which would be resolved by the exposition of Christ as the fulfillment of the priesthood, the temple and sacrifice. No doubt it was this interest which led someone to call the work the epistle to the Hebrews; but the treatment does not suggest to modern scholars that the question was raised by Jewish Christians who wondered about the abolition of the divinely established cultic system of Israel and Judaism. One can see that this could be a genuine problem, but it is not treated expressly elsewhere in the New Testament. Christ is called a priest only in the epistle to the Hebrews, and no officer of the Christian church is called priest, just as the Eucharist is never called a sacrifice. Apparently the problem was not felt, nor was it the problem of the writer of the epistle to the Hebrews.

The epistle is very probably an instance, of rare interest because of its length, of the " teaching " referred to in several books of the New Testament. This teaching is generally understood as the explanation of the Christ event—the saving death and resurrection—in Old Testament terms. The apostolic church claimed to be the fullness of Israel. This claim was vindicated, both in controversy with Jews and in homilies to Christians, by the application of Old Testament texts to the person and life of Jesus. The teaching had not arrived at a standard and uniform structure when the books of the New Testament were written. Where we can trace its content and methods, the teaching was set forth by the technique of interpretation called " rabbinical." Parallels to this technique are found in the rabbinical literature of Judaism, in some instances parallels so close as to be surprising. If Paul had been a student of the rabbis, he would certainly have learned rabbinical interpretation; the New Testament is the best evidence that Paul was not the only Christian who was familiar with rabbinical methods. It appears that the author of the epistle to the Hebrews believed that the explanation of the saving act of Jesus in terms of the Levitical cultic system of sacrifice would enrich the community's understanding of the saving act.

The epistle of James illustrates another area of the teaching which appears much more frequently in the New Testament, the teaching of practical morality. Even the gospels have been expanded by the moral teaching; questions are asked and answered in the gospels which obviously arose from the situation of the early church and its members. Many scholars believe it is next to impossible to reconstruct the moral teaching of Jesus himself, so much has the teaching been expanded. One need not despair to this extent to admit that the teaching has been extremely important in the composition of the gospels.

It is quite clear that the primitive moral teaching of the apostolic church, which must be close to the moral teaching of Jesus, was so radical in character that it furnished genuine problems for a Christian who lived in a Jewish or gentile environment. Jews in gentile cities had met the problem of the exotic Jewish morality by forming their own communities where life under the Law could be lived with less difficulty and without arousing so much hostile comment. Possibly early Christian communities, many of which were largely Jewish, also tended to withdraw into their own quarters; but the New Testament does not recommend this, and such passages as 1 Corinthians 5:9-10 show that Paul did not think of withdrawal as a solution to Christian moral problems. Some knowledge in detail of the Roman Hellenistic world is necessary for the reader to appreciate how violently the Christian ethic departed from the accepted conventions of that world. The modern Christian, it seems, is much less frequently reminded that he deals with people whose scheme of moral values is totally different from the Christian scheme.

This may not be all to the credit of the modern Christian or the modern world. The historian must judge soberly that public morality, at least, is much less offensive to Christian morality than the public morality of the Roman world; the modern world has in the course of centuries incorporated a considerable amount of Christian ethics in its laws and customs. But the modern church has also accommodated itself to a number of features of the secular ethic which are openly or covertly anti-Christian. We are not in the situation of the early Christians, when the moral revolution of the gospel was confronted with a society remarkably immoral. Hostility was inevitable; it is one notable feature of the New Testament books that they do not encourage Christians to hasten what is inevitable.

The solution of the moral problems of the Christian swimming in a pagan sea was not reached by compromise of any Christian principle. The Christian is not advised to preserve his Christian morality by thanking God that he is better than his neighbor, nor by fostering that kind of self-righteousness and sense of superiority which is traditionally called pharisaic. Our own moral judgments are so often clouded by complications from the world which we think we cannot simplify that the raw confrontation of the New Testament should help us. Again, one needs some knowledge of the Hellenistic-Roman world to recognize that we are unfair to the apostolic Christians if we think they faced their moral problems in an uncomplicated world. They did not think that complication was an excuse for not facing the problem.

JOHN L. McKENZIE, S.J.

The Epistle to the Hebrews

INTRODUCTION

Even in the early church, the Epistle to the Hebrews was always regarded as an unusual document. It is almost as long as the Epistle to the Romans, yet, despite its length and the depth of its theological insights, it was constantly overshadowed by the Pauline epistles. It was only after a hard struggle that it was accepted into the canon of the New Testament. Today no one would dispute its status as a canonical book, but it still impresses the reader as an unusual piece of writing.

There are various reasons for the way in which the Epistle to the Hebrews was neglected and for the inaccurate opinion people had of it. Even the title " To the Hebrews " implies that, at the time when the epistles of the New Testament were being formed into a collection, nothing was known about the real circumstances of its origin. In the New Testament, the name " Hebrews " meant Aramaic-speaking Jewish-Christians (2 Cor. 11:22; Phil. 3:5; Acts 6:1), or at least those who had been born Jews. In the early church, this gave rise to the belief that the Epistle to the Hebrews must have been written in Aramaic originally. However, this opinion has long since been abandoned; it is now acknowledged that the epistle was originally composed in Greek. Indeed, it displays a high degree of stylistic elegance and literary ability. Consequently, it could not have been destined for the Jewish-Christians of Palestine, even if most of them were, in fact, bilingual.

Modern commentators are not even sure that the epistle was addressed to a Jewish-Christian church. The author consistently quotes the Bible in the Greek translation, the Septuagint; gentile-Christians would be familiar with this. As is clear from the baptismal catechesis (6:1-2), those to whom the epistle was addressed had to be instructed about "faith in God" and the "resurrection of the dead and the eternal judgment."

If the recipients of the letter were gentiles (or people who had been born of Christian parents), and not converts from Judaism, another widely accepted theory also falls away. This is that the author's purpose was to warn his readers against reverting to Judaism. According to this theory, the Christians of Palestine were tempted to abandon their new faith and return to the religion of their fathers, because of the magnificence and splendor of the temple worship. Such a far-fetched explanation of the purpose of the epistle could only arise from a superficial and biased reading of it. There is not a single passage which speaks of reverting to Judaism; nor is there any reference to Herod's temple. On the contrary, the problems confronting the readers of the epistle are of a completely different nature, and the author tries to solve them by his theological reflections. These are: (1) The fact that salvation was not yet a visible reality; (2) Moral weakness, and (3) The hostility of the world.

(1) The fact that their salvation had not yet been fully revealed must have constituted an ever more pressing problem for the various local churches towards the end of the first century. Why was it that the promises concerning the coming of God's kingdom and the Lord's appearing had not been fulfilled? Was the hope of a glorious world to come an idle and vain hope after all? We can be sure that the postponement of the parousia in itself rarely led to a complete loss of faith. However, it may be that at that time, as in our own day, there was considerable doubt, uncertainty, discontent, and disillusionment among so-

called good Christians. People still clung fast to the rule of faith and the various professions of faith which had been handed down, but they no longer experienced the same joy, confidence (*parrhesia*: 3:6; 4:16; 10:19, 35), or " full certainty " (*plaerophoria*: 6:11; 10:22). The proclamation of the gospel met with bored indifference or even rejection (cf. 2:3; 4:1-2; 5:11; 12:25); some Christians had already begun to stay away from the liturgical assembly (10:25). Abandoning the church completely and " falling away from the living God " (3:12; cf. 6:6; 10:26-29; 12:15-17) would mean only a small step further.

The author of the letter realized that it would not be enough merely to repeat ancient and venerable truths to overcome this crisis of faith. On the other hand, it is quite clear that he could not challenge truths which the church had believed and taught since its earliest days, nor had he any wish to do so. Like the preachers and missionaries who went before him, he too speaks of the second coming of Christ (9:28) and says that " the day is near " (10:25); he cites Habakkuk's words about the " very, very little while " which remains before this event, and assures his readers that " he who is coming will come and will not delay " (10:37). It is true that we need " patience " (6:12) and " endurance " (10:36; 12:1), if we are to inherit God's promise like the Old Testament witnesses to the faith.

However, we can be sure that the readers of the letter were already familiar with these ideas, and they do not form the heart of the letter, theologically speaking. In their minds, the idea that the parousia must soon occur at some point in time had become questionable. Consequently the author, who was an accomplished philosopher, chooses instead the spatial and metaphysical idea of an earthly and a heavenly world. Like the Jewish religious thinker and philosopher, Philo of Alexandria (*c.* 20 B.C.

to *c.* A.D. 50), he divides reality into two spheres, an earthly, shadowy, and ephemeral world, and a heavenly, real, and eternal world. The earthly world is only an image of the heavenly reality which is its prototype. This Platonist idea proved to be of real value in explaining the meaning of the saving events of the New Testament. This meaning is quite independent of the question concerning the time when these events will be fully accomplished. With its law, its cult, and its priesthood, the Old Testament is inextricably bound up with the visible, earthly, and transitory world. Christ, on the other hand, came as the " high priest of the real blessings " (9:11) (that is, of the heavenly blessings, of which all earthly blessings are only a shadow). The sacrifice of atonement he offered on the cross opened the way into God's true holy of holies; the faithful already possess the " true image of these realities " (10:1); they can now enter the heavenly sanctuary, God's presence, in his grace (4:16; 10:19–22; 12:22–24). Therefore, the idea that their salvation had not yet been revealed, which caused the faithful so much distress, was based on a false interpretation of the facts. It is not the visible realities of this earth which are important; it is the lasting blessings of heaven, and these are invisible (ch. 11). It is true that " we do not yet see " how the world to come is already subject to man (2:8). But the promise of universal sovereignty has already been fulfilled in Jesus (1:2); and " we already see " him " crowned with glory and honor " (2:9). The man who has faith is convinced of the existence of what is invisible (11:1); he holds fast by what he cannot see, " as if he saw it " (11:27).

The heavenly blessings, the " powers of the world to come," can already be experienced interiorly (6:4–5). In the same way, Christian faith enjoys an insight into the secrets of the heavenly world. There it sees the blessings which were conferred on Jesus in accordance with God's promise, his enthronement as Son and Redeemer, and the honor and glory with which he was crowned. But how do the " eyes of faith " know about what has happened in heaven? First and foremost from the teaching of scripture. For the Epistle to the Hebrews, scripture is an illustrated representation of invisible events; it recounts the mysterious words God addresses to his Son; in it, the Son speaks to God. It seems, however, that such an exegesis would have been possible only where the invisible events of heaven already occupied a firm place in the faith of the local Christian community. The heavenly high priest, the Son who is enthroned at God's right hand, could be held up before the eyes of the faithful only in a situation in which people realized they were in his presence, in virtue of the profession of faith they made in the liturgy. His exaltation would have to be celebrated as something present and actual in the liturgical use of scripture. In such circumstances, the use of expressions such as " seeing," " touching," " enjoying " with reference to the world to come would be meaningful.

The author was anxious to convince his readers of the certainty of the hope they entertained in faith. Therefore, we could say that he had to enable them to see the saving blessings which are to come for themselves; they have to have almost a personal experience of them. Consequently, he exhorts them to show greater eagerness in listening to God's words in sermons and in scripture readings (1:1—4:13); to approach the throne of grace in the heavenly sanctuary with confidence (4:14—10:31); and to assure themselves of a heavenly reward by enduring trials and suffering (10:32—13:17). These exhortations correspond roughly with the sections into which the letter is divided. They also provide its readers with the means to overcome their weakness in moral matters and maintain a bold front before a hostile world.

(2) The longer Christians had to wait for their redemption to be fully accomplished the more obvious it became that they were not immune to moral weakness. Strictly speaking, there should have been no such thing as sin among Christians, once they had been baptized. However, the facts spoke louder than any theories. We know from other sources dating from the end of the apostolic era that the sins of Christians constituted a problem, not merely for the penitential discipline of the church, but also for theological reflection. The Epistle to the Hebrews distinguishes three types of sins: (a) Transgressions committed before baptism, " in the time of the first covenant "; (b) Sins of frailty and ignorance committed by those who were already Christians; (c) The deliberate and unforgivable sin of apostasy from the Christian faith. On a pastoral level, the epistle is aimed primarily at remedying the weakness in moral matters from which its readers suffered; this must not be allowed to degenerate into hopeless apostasy. Yet, the theoretical question concerning the forgiveness of sin by the shedding of Jesus' blood occupies a large place. Of course, these theological reflections also serve the author's pastoral aim.

(a) At baptism, the faithful received the forgiveness of all the " transgressions " which " were committed during the time of the first covenant " (9:15). Jesus' blood " purified " their consciences " from lifeless deeds," so that they could now " serve the living God " (9:14; cf. 10:2). This purification of conscience, therefore, also had a positive aspect; it made Christians capable of sharing in the worship offered in the heavenly sanctuary. This becomes even more clear in the idea of " sanctification " (2:11;

9:13; 10:10.14.29; 13:12). Anyone who has been sanctified is consecrated; he is set apart from all that is earthly and profane and dedicated to God's service. However, a certain amount of tension still remains; by his sacrifice, Christ has " sanctified us once and for all " (10:10), and yet we must still acquire a share in God's sanctity by enduring the strict discipline of obedience (12:10). On the other hand, only those who are God's sons are worthy to receive this discipline (12:8). If we had not already been sanctified to some degree, we should scarcely be capable of striving for sanctity (12:14).

In addition to the concepts of " purification " and " sanctification," the Epistle to the Hebrews also uses the idea of " bringing to perfection (completion)," an idea which is peculiar to this epistle, to describe the heavenly and definitive character of the forgiveness of sins. The earthly and figurative sacrifices of the old law could not " bring " those who offered them " to completion, where conscience was concerned " (9:9; 10:1). Only Jesus could " bring those who had been sanctified to completion, once and for all " (10:14), by means of the unique offering of his body. What does this mean? Certainly it is not just a question of the psychological conviction that our consciences are set at rest and find their peace with God through faith in the atoning power of the cross. What our author has in mind is rather an ontological reality. God's Son achieved his complete status by being raised from the agony and humiliation of death to the heavenly sanctuary (5:7–10). In the same way, the faithful are brought to completion by being delivered from the bondage of death and Satan through Jesus' death (2:14–15), and transferred into God's saving kingdom. The achievement of his perfect status for Jesus meant, at the same time, that he was consecrated as the heavenly high priest; similarly, the Christian community is consecrated for the priestly ministry in the heavenly sanctuary.

It was not merely the love of theological speculation that led our author to go into such detail in describing the " greater promise " which is involved in the forgiveness of sins (8:6.12). More than anything else, he wanted to help the faithful to recover the joyful consciousness of their sublime dignity as ministers of the new covenant. By means of Jesus' blood, God had purified them, sanctified them, and brought them to completion or perfection. This was a unique blessing, conferred once and for all, and it should have been a constant cause for grateful acknowledgement, as Christians " approached the throne of grace with confidence " (4:16; 10:19–22). It was here, in the course of the liturgical assembly, that the threatened and persecuted church could most easily have recourse to the help of its heavenly high priest.

(b) The faithful have been purified from sin once and for all. Consequently, they can never more be conscious of such a sin as would involve the anguish of separation from God or open and obstinate revolt against him. Their present situation, therefore, is characterized by the term weakness (4:15). This concept includes a whole range of states, from the state of " being tempted " (2:8; 4:15) to flirting with sin, which is bound to obstruct the athlete in his efforts and turn him aside from his goal (12:1) by the practice of cunning and deceit (3:13). The hands of Christians were already becoming slack; their knees were beginning to flag and their feet to stumble, as their legs threatened to go from under them (12:12–13). From the biblical imagery of these phrases we can, of course, draw no conclusions concerning the particular sins of frailty in the church which the author had in mind. In particular, we cannot simply take our distinction between mortal and venial sins from the moral

theology books and read it into the Epistle to the Hebrews. For
the Epistle to the Hebrews, every sin committed by a Christian
is " venial," that is, it can always be repaired with the help of
the merciful and compassionate high priest (2:18; 4:15; 5:2;
7:25; 9:24), as long as the Christian has not abandoned his faith
completely. The epistle does not recognize any organized
penitential discipline in the church. Yet, it already contains the
essential elements of the sacrament of penance as it is found
later, the efficacious intercession of the heavenly high priest,
fraternal correction and mutual help in the church by means of
exhortations (3:12; 10:5) and watchfulness (12:15), and finally
the self-evident obligation of each Christian to pick himself up
once more and " walk with unwavering steps " (12:13).

(c) Encouraging references to the means of salvation are not
the only device the epistle uses in its attempt to remedy the
" weakness " from which the community suffered; it also employs decisive and earnest warnings against the danger of an
apostasy which would be irreparable. The rigor of the repeated
warnings (2:2-3; 3:12-13; 4:1; 6:4-8; 10:26-31; 12:12-17)
has often shocked readers of the epistle and earned the author
the reputation of being a harsh and inexorable prophet of doom.
This impression could only spring from failure to interpret what
he says in the light of the context. The threats are directed at
Christians who were in danger, to prevent them from taking
the last fateful step; they are not meant for those who had
already fallen away and were perhaps now inquiring about the
possibility of doing penance and being readmitted to the community. The question of what was to be done about apostates
who were repentant belonged to a later age; our author did not
have to consider it. If he had been confronted with this problem

in his capacity as a pastor, he would probably have given a more balanced reply and one which set no limits to God's mercy.

(3) Listlessness in matters of faith and moral weakness must have been particularly dangerous, if Christians also had to endure the world's hostility in their own persons. It is not clear from the letter whether the community was faced with a persecution in the strict sense. There had been a persecution in the past, soon after the church was founded. The author says that his readers had endured slander, oppression, imprisonment, and the confiscation of their property (10:32-34). He says nothing about anyone having been martyred, but it is possible that those who had established the church and preached God's word to his readers had died a violent death (13:7). The exhortation, " You have not yet resisted to the point of bloodshed, in your fight against sin " (12:4), may imply that the community would soon be faced with a life and death struggle. Other passages would also be easier to explain if we suppose that the letter was written on the eve of the persecution of Domitian. This may be the reason why chapter 11 ends with an extremely realistic description of the martyrs and persecutions of the Old Testament (11:35-38). It may also explain why the author feels compelled to prove the necessity and significance of suffering and chastisement from scripture (12:5-11). For the same reason, at the end of his letter, he calls upon his readers to " go out to " Jesus crucified and " bear his shame " (13:13; cf. 11:26; 12:2).

It is possible that what the author has in mind in this letter is not persecution from without, but only the ordinary sufferings and hardships of everyday life, the " being in the body " (13:3). Even in that case, however, there can be no doubt that fear of death (2:15; cf. 5:7; 11:13) and reluctance to endure suffering (12:3-11) were undermining the community's confidence. It was

not really the scandal of Christ's cross (1 Cor. 1:23) which was
the cause of the difficulties the readers of the epistle encountered
in their faith. Rather, they felt that they had been deceived in
their hope, because they foresaw that they would have to endure
death—and perhaps a painful and bloody death. This interpretation makes it easier to see why the author lays such emphasis on
the inevitability of man's fatal destiny (2:14–15; 9:27; 11:13);
he returns again and again to the saving efficacy of Christ's
bloody death (2:9–10.14.18; 5:7–10; 7:27; 9:11–28; 10:5–14.
19–21; 12:2–3.24; 13:12.20). St. Paul, in his earlier letters, had
reckoned with the possibility that he and other Christians might
still be alive at the time of the parousia (1 Thess. 14:15.17;
1 Cor. 15:51–52). The Epistle to the Hebrews, on the other
hand, openly supposes that death is inevitable as a means of
attaining salvation. Jesus " attained his completion " through
his passion and death; in other words, it was through his passion
and death that he entered the true holy of holies, to take his place
at God's right hand. In the same way, " the souls of the just who
have attained their completion " (12:23) have already entered
the heavenly Jerusalem. The faithful have been sanctified and
brought to perfection by Jesus' blood; they have no need to fear
death any more. When their human destiny has been fulfilled
(9:27), they will follow their " leader " (2:10; 12:2) and
" precursor " (6:20), the " great shepherd of the sheep " (13:
20), into the heavenly country, God's eternal city (11:14–16;
12:22; 13:14).

The difficulties and problems which beset the Christians at
the end of the first century are not all that much different from
those which so often make the road to God laborious and
difficult for us. Once we have realized this, the Epistle to the
Hebrews begins to have meaning for us. It exhorts and instructs

us; it holds a promise for us, while at the same time it warns, threatens, and implores us. It is true that not all the ideas and proofs cited by the author will have the same appeal for us. Then we must ask ourselves how we are to approach those who have become listless and unsure of themselves in our own day, and this means in the first place our own souls which have become so tired (12:3). God's word must once more prove itself " alive and effective, sharper than any two-edged sword " (4:12).

OUTLINE

GOD'S PROMISE IN HIS SON (1:1—4:13)

I. Listen eagerly to God's Word: it has come to us through the Son, not through angels (1:1—2:4)
   1. The history of revelation in the Old Testament (1:1)
   2. The Son has preached to us (1:2)
   3. The Son is enthroned in heaven (1:3–13)
   4. The service the angels perform (1:14)
   5. An urgent warning not to reject the salvation proclaimed by Jesus and the apostles (2:1–4)

II. As God's sons and brothers of Christ, we must hold fast to our first confidence and the hope which is our boast (2:5—3:6)
   1. The right to rule over the world to come has been promised to men, not to angels (2:5–8)
   2. The promise contained in Psalm 8 has already been fulfilled in Jesus, but by way of suffering and death (2:9–10)
   3. Christ and his brothers—the liturgical community of heaven (2:11–13)
   4. Man's destiny is to die; God's Son takes this on himself (2:14–15)
   5. Our High Priest is faithful and compassionate; he atones for sin and helps those who are tempted (2:16–18)
   6. Look at Jesus, the Faithful Apostle and High Priest who, as God's Son, is Head of his household (3:1–6)

III. Do not harden your hearts against God's call and his promise (3:7—4:13)
1. A quotation from Psalm 95:7-11 (3:7-11)
2. A warning against disbelief and sin (3:12-14)
3. This warning is meant only for the disobedient (3:15—4:2)
4. God's rest and his six days' work (4:3-5)
5. A final exhortation (4:6-11)
6. A hymn to the Word of God which has power over life and death (4:12-13)

JESUS' HIGH PRIESTHOOD (4:14—10:31)
I. Jesus, our High Priest, the Son of God (4:14—5:10)
1. We have a High Priest who can sympathize with us (4:14—5:3)
2. Our High Priest received his vocation from God and owes his appointment to him (5:4-10)

II. A digression: the state of the community (5:11—6:20)
1. The recipients of the epistle are like children (5:11-14)
2. A beginner's catechism and a word for the initiates (6:1-3)
3. A warning against irreparable apostasy (6:4-8)
4. There is good hope of improvement (6:9-12)
5. Abraham and the divinely guaranteed promise (6:13-20)

III. Jesus' Melchizedekian priesthood (7:1-28)
1. Melchizedek the priest-king (7:1-3)
2. Melchizedek is greater than Abraham or Levi (7:4-10)
3. The priesthood and the law (7:11-19)
4. The guarantee of a better covenant (7:20-25)
5. A hymn of praise to the heavenly High Priest (7:26-28)

IV. Priest and mediator of a new covenant (8:1—10:18)
  1. A priest in the heavenly sanctuary (8:1–5)
  2. Mediator of a better covenant (8:6–13)
  3. The earthly sanctuary (9:1–5)
  4. The priestly ministry in the earthly tent (9:6–10)
  5. Christ's priestly ministry in heaven (9:11–14)
  6. The testator's death (9:15–17)
  7. The blood of the covenant (9:18–22)
  8. A unique and better sacrifice (9:23–28)
  9. The shadow and the archetype (10:1–4)
  10. The offering of Christ's body (10:5–10)
  11. Christ's sacrifice is final and cannot be repeated (10:11–18)

V. An exhortation and a warning (10:19–31)
  1. Let us approach (10:19–22)
  2. We must hold fast by what we profess (10:23–25)
  3. A terrible judgment threatens those who fall away (10:26–31)

CONSTANCY IN TRIALS AND PERSECUTION (10:32—13:25)

I. A call to fight for the faith (10:32—12:1)
  1. Remember the distress of earlier days (10:32–39)
  2. A digression: models of faith (11:1—12:3)
    a) A definition of faith (11:1–2)
    b) The creation of the aeons (11:3)
    c) Abel the just (11:4)
    d) How Enoch was taken away (11:5–6)
    e) Noah and the ark (11:7)
    f) Abraham's pilgrimage in faith (11:8–10)
    g) The promise of offspring (11:11–12)

h) The heavenly country (11 : 13–16)

i) The sacrifice of Isaac (11 : 17–19)

j) The patriarchs' blessings (11 : 20–22)

k) Moses' example of faith (11 : 23–28)

l) Examples of miraculous escapes and earthly success (11 : 29–35a)

m) The martyrs of the old covenant (11 : 35b–38)

n) Concluding remarks concerning the martyrs (11 : 39–40)

o) The Author and Completer of faith (12 : 1–3)

3. God's wisdom in training us (12 : 4–11)

4. Sharing pastoral responsibility (12 : 12–17)

5. Judgment and grace (12 : 18–29)

6. An exhortation to live a Christian life (13 : 1–6)

7. Orthodoxy in the faith, courage in suffering, true worship, and obedience to the church (13 : 7–17)

8. Conclusion: a request for prayers, a final blessing, an exhortation, news of Timothy, and farewell (13 : 18–25)

GOD'S PROMISE IN HIS SON
(1:1—4:13)

The letter opens with a brief glance at the history of God's word in
the Old Testament. Then it goes on to celebrate the praises of the
Son who has brought God's final and definitive offer of salvation.
By being enthroned in heaven, he has been raised to an incomparably
more exalted dignity than the angels. Anyone who disregards the
salvation he proclaimed deserves a far more frightful punishment
than those who transgressed the law which was given by angels
(1:1—2:4). The theme of the message of salvation which is preached
is the world to come. This world will be governed not by angels but
by men, that is, by God's only-begotten Son and his adopted sons.
That is why the Son took flesh and blood and became a high priest
for his brothers (2:5-18). If we hold fast to our faith to the end,
without being shaken, we will enter the heavenly resting place as
God's household and Christ's companions. On the other hand, those
who refuse belief are threatened with the same disaster as the disobedient Israelites suffered in the wilderness (3:1—4:11). A hymn
to God's word which has the power of life and death closes the first
part of the letter (4:12-13).

Listen Eagerly to God's Word:
It has Come to Us Through the Son, Not Through
Angels (1:1—2:4)

The first lengthy section is intended to rouse us to pay more and
more attention to the New Testament message of salvation. As
we learn from a reproachful remark which occurs in a later
passage, the Christians to whom the author was speaking had

become " hard of hearing " (5:11). God's word had lost the charm of novelty for them; it was no longer worth listening to. They were second-generation Christians (2:3). Many of them had probably joined in the liturgical assembly from their earliest days and listened to innumerable sermons. We may ask whether the exhortatory sermon (13:22) contained in the Epistle to the Hebrews succeeded in curing their deep-seated indifference and making them listen to God's word once more. And their indifference is ours also.

The History of Revelation in the Old Testament (1:1)

¹*God spoke to the fathers of old through the prophets on many occasions and in many ways.*

The " letter " opens without any form of address or greeting; there is no expression of thanks and the author offers no prayer. In other words, the various forms of politeness common in antiquity are missing. From the very first words, the letter appears as an appeal which is intended to make its hearers listen. But is the appeal contained in this first half sentence really so inspiring? Do we not rather get the impression that the author's carefully chosen alliteration is intended to express the monotony and boredom many Christians felt, when they were reminded of the prophetic writings of the Old Testament? That had all been told to " the fathers," and " of old " at that. What difference did it make to us now? In any case, who could make head or tail of the " multiplicity " of Old Testament texts? It is true, of course, that it was the same God, our God, who then spoke by the prophets. But surely his word had accommodated itself only too

well to the multiplicity of human words which are mutually
contradictory and tend to eliminate one another by their very
multiplicity? It would seem utterly impossible that God's will
for us could be deduced in obligatory fashion from the Old
Testament alone. The first half sentence of the letter, therefore,
does nothing but raise problem after problem for the reader.
These are the problems which the letter will now presumably
go on to answer.

The Son has Preached to Us (1:2)

²*But at the end of these days, he spoke to us in the Son whom
he has appointed to inherit everything, through whom he created
the aeons.*

It was not only to the fathers that God spoke; neither was it only
in the dim and distant past. His word has also come to us, that
is, to the Christian churches, and this is his final and definitive
word in which all that is still to come is already present. This
divine word has the power of life and death (cf. 4:12–13), and
it was not a multitude of spokesmen or anonymous prophets
who brought it to us; it was God's only Son himself. The author
is clearly referring to the unique historical fact of Jesus' preaching (cf. 2:3), although he says nothing about its content. His
readers or hearers were familiar with Jesus' teaching from the
catechesis and probably from one or other of the gospels. They
knew what he had promised his disciples, and the demands he
made of them. In fact, it was precisely because they were so
familiar with all this that they might be inclined to see nothing

extraordinary in what Jesus said. We, too, will find it difficult to see anything divine in the simple, straightforward, and almost " banal " (K. Barth) counsels of the gospel, if we forget who it was that gave them.

For this reason, the letter immediately adds a whole series of exalted titles which are to be applied to Christ. These make it clear in advance that what the Son has to say to us must be important. He is the Heir of all. He will inherit us—and it will be for him to decide what we are worth. He is the mediator of creation; it was through him that God created the aeons, the present and the future world. After God, therefore, it is to him that we owe our existence. The origin and the goal of all being, what is present and what is to come, are determined by Jesus, the Son of God. We must be careful not to take our faith in this too much for granted.

The Son is Enthroned in Heaven (1 : 3–13)

³*He is the splendor of his glory, the true image of his being. He upholds all things by the word of his power, and now that he has brought purification from sin, he has taken his place on high at the right of [God's] majesty.* ⁴*He is all the more powerful than the angels as the name he has inherited is superior to them.* ⁵*To which of the angels did he [God] ever say: " You are my Son. I begot you today " (Ps. 2:7)? and again: " I will be a father to him, and he will be my Son " (2 Sam. 7:14)?* ⁶*But when he will bring the First-Born into the world once more, he says: "And all God's angels must pay him homage " (Ps. 97:7).* ⁷*To the angels he says: " He makes his angels like the winds, and his servants as flames of fire " (Ps. 104:4).* ⁸*But to the Son*

*he says: " Your throne, O God, lasts for ever and ever, and the
scepter of justice is the scepter of his kingship. ⁹You loved justice
and hated wickedness. And so God, your God, has anointed you
with the oil of great rejoicing before your companions" (Ps.
45:7–8). ¹⁰And: " You have laid the foundations of the earth
at the beginning, Lord, and the heavens are the work of your
hands. ¹¹They will vanish into nothingness, but you remain.
They will all grow old like clothes; you will roll them up like a
cloak, ¹²like a garment, and they will be changed. But you remain unchanged; your years will never end" (Ps. 102:26–28).
¹³Indeed, to which of the angels did he ever say: " Sit at my
right hand, and I will make your enemies a footstool for your
feet" (Ps. 110:1)?*

It is clear that the author realized it would not be enough to
speak about Christ in abstract terms, particularly as what he had
to say concerned Christ's place in the events which preceded,
and which will follow, the world's history. If a person wants to
inspire faith in another, or enkindle it once more, he must tell
the " story " of Jesus; he must recall what Jesus has done for us.
Nowadays, we should probably prefer to listen to a simple
historical account of Jesus' life. However, the author of the letter
had been formed in the Alexandrine school and he chooses to
present his ideas in the form of a solemn hymn which we could
describe as a theme from the heavenly liturgy. The subject of his
hymn is not the exterior events of Jesus' life which were known
both to his readers and to us; instead, he speaks of the events of
the heavenly world in which Jesus was enthroned as Son of God
and Ruler of the World. These events can be perceived only
with the eyes and ears of faith. In their construction, these verses
bear a close resemblance to the famous hymn of the Epistle to

the Philippians. There, too, Jesus' earthly ministry is set in a framework made up of his eternal preëxistence and his heavenly exaltation. The Christ-hymn of Philippians 2 describes the way he followed as a sort of parabola which descends steeply from his eternal, divine mode of being and reaches its lowest point in the cross, before ascending once more into the sublimity of the God-head. In the Epistle to the Hebrews, on the contrary, Christ's humiliation is scarcely attended to any more. The path he followed to death on the cross, by means of which he " effected the purification of sins," is portrayed as the solemn approach of the heavenly high priest to God's throne.

In reality—the reality which is visible only to faith—Jesus of Nazareth was a divine being. He was endowed with the attributes which Alexandrine Judaism predicated of eternal Wisdom. He was the " splendor of the divine glory "; " the true image of his being " who " upholds all things by the word of his power " (cf. Wis. 7:25–26). It is better not to interpret this threefold description of Christ's being in the light of the more precise norms of later Christology. We should regard them as an attempt to link Jesus' person and his ministry as closely as possible with God.

This desire is also at the root of the protracted comparison between Christ and the angels. Of course, it may also be that the church to which this epistle is addressed paid an exaggerated cult to the angels, like the church at Colossae (cf. Col. 2:18). In this passage, however, the angels serve primarily as a scenic background to the author's description of Christ's enthronement. For an Oriental ruler, ascending the throne involved three stages: (1) The adoption of the new king by God, who gave him a new name; (2) The homage paid to the new king by the local nobility (in this case, the angels); (3) The handing over of the right to rule (scepter, anointing, ascent of the throne). No great proof is needed to show that this was the type of ceremony the author had in mind when he searched scripture to find what he thought were suitable passages. It is clear that he regarded the Old Testament as a closed and secret book in which we can read about the liturgical and eschatological drama of Christ's enthronement in heaven. If we want to understand the Epistle to the Hebrews, we must make this way of interpreting—or, better, of accommodating—scripture our own.

Hebrews 1:1-12 is read as the first lesson in the third Mass on Christmas day. The principal reason why it was chosen is certainly verse 6: " When he will bring the First-Born into the world again, he says: ' And all God's angels must adore him.' " The church looked on these words as a confirmation of the story of Jesus' birth, where we are told the angels paid him homage in the fields at Bethlehem (Lk. 2:13-14), but we must remember that what the epistle is thinking of primarily is Christ's exaltation and his second coming.

The Service the Angels Perform (1:14)

14Have not all these " liturgical " spirits been sent to serve, for the benefit of those who are to inherit salvation?

We have just mentioned the possibility that the readers of the epistle were inclined to indulge in an unhealthy cult of the angels. We cannot be sure that this is true; it may be that the author himself merely wished to be clear about the angels' role in salvation. In any case, the present verse, with its rhetorical question, certainly expresses a fundamental, not to say a revolu-

tionary, fact. This statement must not be taken merely as a proof
for the traditional doctrine of guardian angels as if, in such a
multiplicity of angels, there must be some who are devoted to
the lowly and not very respected role of being guardian angels.
On the contrary, the passage speaks about " all " spirits; it includes, therefore, archangels, thrones, dominations, and any
other name we may choose to call the most exalted inhabitants of
heaven. But even this doctrine, which teaches that all the angels
without exception are devoted to our protection and service,
would not be really exciting if we did not realize that the angels
are beings who have control over great sectors of creation. In a
pre- or post-Christian world (understood in a theological and not
in a historical sense), the angels arrogate authority over men to
themselves. They demand that men should spend their lives for
their greater glory. But Christ has deprived these powers of
their absolute authority; now they are obliged to serve mankind
and promote their salvation. We should not imagine that these
are just empty thoughts. If ideas and the different spheres of
reality are in the service of man, his position is obviously much
happier than that of a person who must sacrifice himself for an
idea, an institution, or an abstract order of some kind.

*An Urgent Warning Not to Reject the Salvation Proclaimed by
Jesus and the Apostles (2 : 1–4)*

¹*For this reason, it is necessary that we should attend all the more
earnestly to what we have heard, so that we may not be carried
away.* ²*Indeed, if the word spoken by angels was valid, so that
transgressing it or turning a deaf ear to it in any way was duly
requited,* ³*how can we hope to escape, we who have paid no*

attention to such salvation as this? This salvation takes its origin from the Lord's own preaching; it was officially communicated to us by those who heard him. ⁴Here, too, God added his testimony with signs and wonders and varied acts of power, and the outpourings of the Holy Spirit, in accordance with his will.

We must remember that the mysterious account of Christ's enthronement was only a digression, an excursus, which interrupted the principal theme, the revelation God has made us in his Son in this last stage of time. Therefore, in calling on readers or listeners of this verse to pay more attention to the message of salvation which is preached, the letter is merely returning to its real theme, which it now brings to a conclusion. Here, for the first time, we see the extraordinary technique in which the Old and the New Testaments are contrasted. The " word spoken by angels," that is, the law, corresponds to " the salvation preached by the Lord "; transgressing the law and turning a deaf ear to it are paralleled by the indifference and neglect shown by Christians. From a moral viewpoint, transgressing the law might be a much more serious offense than a Christian's indifference to the message of salvation. It is precisely among lukewarm and free-thinking Christians that we often find exceedingly upright and good men who go to great lengths to avoid any gross violation of the moral law. The Epistle to the Hebrews does not deny this, but it maintains that a man who abandons the gospel or loses interest in the faith runs an incomparably greater risk of failing to attain the whole goal of his life. He may be carried away, like a swimmer trying to cross a river in flood who fails to reach the safety of the opposite bank. But why is it so terribly important to try to reach the opposite bank? Would it not be better simply to let oneself be carried away by the stream of fate? Anyone who talks like that regards the faith which brings salvation as an illusion; he sees sin and death as inevitable events with which we must come to terms.

As God's Sons and Brothers of Christ, We Must Hold Fast to Our First Confidence and the Hope Which is Our Boast (2:5—3:6)

The Right to Rule over the World to Come Has Been Promised to Men, Not to Angels (2 : 5–8)

⁵*It is not to the angels that he has subjected the world to come of which we are speaking.* ⁶*On the contrary, someone tells us in a certain passage: " What is man, that you should take thought of him, or a son of man, that you should watch over him?* ⁷*For a short time, you humbled him beneath the angels. You crowned him with glory and honor.* ⁸*You have put everything under his feet* " (Ps. 8 : 5–7). *The words " subjected everything " mean that he has left nothing which is not subjected to him. But, at the moment, we see that everything is not yet subject to him.*

The epistle is about to discuss the world to come. It does not do this in a spirit of vain curiosity. The Jewish and Christian apocalypses were intent on exploring God's secrets and the secrets of his heavenly world; the Epistle to the Hebrews, on the contrary, is concerned with the active faith of its readers who had become tired and were given to doubting. Therefore, the names and images which are used to describe the object of the promise —God's household, God's rest, the true sanctuary, the heavenly country, the future city—could all be changed, once the faithful realize that their efforts in this world, their suffering, and even death itself, are not in vain.

Another trait which distinguishes the teaching of the Epistle to the Hebrews concerning the world to come from many current conceptions concerning the same subject is the human character of the salvation which awaits us. The world to come was planned not for angels, but for men; it was made for men. No one can say, therefore, that what the faith promises us is a far off and alien world of spirits where only angels and saints could feel at home. The inspired words of Psalm 8, which is a hymn to man's glory, are meant for all of us poor earth-dwellers who feel lost when confronted with the limitless expanse of the universe. For all his limited knowledge of the world and of nature, the psalmist is filled with reverent amazement at the thought that the God who had created such marvels, and set the sun, the moon, and the stars in the vault of heaven, should still have a thought for man, who is so insignificant. Surely we today have far more reason to reflect anew on man's place in the cosmos. The fantastic successes of the space age have demonstrated man's insecurity in spectacular fashion, showing that he is not really at home in this present world. Where is this " world to come " in which everything is really subject to man? The salvation promised in God's word is nowhere to be seen as yet.

The Promise Contained in Psalm 8 has Already Been Fulfilled in Jesus, but by Way of Suffering and Death (2 : 9–10)

⁹*But we see Jesus, who was humbled beneath the angels for a short time, crowned with glory and honor, because of his suffer-*

*ing and death. By God's grace, he was to taste death for every-
one. ¹⁰It was fitting, indeed, that God—for whom and through
whom [is] everything—who was determined to lead many sons
to glory, should bring to perfection by means of suffering the
One who was to lead them to salvation.*

The invisible character of our salvation is not absolute. For those
who believe, there is something which can be " seen " already,
Jesus' cross and his exaltation. The author sees Jesus' history,
his entry into the glory of heaven through humiliation, foretold
in Psalm 8. He is able to interpret the psalm in this way because
he substitutes a phrase with a temporal meaning (" For a short
time ") for the words of the original text (" A little less than the
angels ") which have a qualitative sense. Such an interpretation,
however, presupposes that Jesus represents mankind in general.
He is our " prototype "; his destiny is intended to be typical of
all men. It shows us the lines the destiny of all men will follow.
No one can remain indifferent to what has happened to Jesus.
Each one of us shares a community of being and destiny with him
from which no one can withdraw. This truth is a source of
encouragement for Christians who are faced with suffering and
persecution. The very factors which, humanly speaking, oppress
and torment them also inspire them with the certainty of the
salvation which is to come.

*Christ and His Brothers—
the Liturgical Community of Heaven (2 : 11–13)*

¹¹*For the One who makes holy and those who are made holy all
[come] from the same stock. For this reason, he is not ashamed
to call them " brothers," ¹²saying: " I will make his name*

known to my brothers. I will praise you in the midst of the congregation " (Ps. 22:23). [13]*And again: " I will be one who has put his trust in him* " (Is. 8:17). *And again: " See, here am I and the children God has given me* " (Is. 8:18).

The community which exists between Jesus who " makes holy " and sinful men who need to be made holy is based on their common origin from God. God's only-begotten Son and his adopted sons are brothers from all eternity. Underlying these mysterious words, with all that they imply, we catch a glimpse of the basic idea of the whole letter—the faithful as a liturgical community which approaches God's throne under the leadership of Jesus its high priest. It is good to know that the Saviour who takes away our sins and frees us from the fear of death is our brother. And, although he has good reason to be ashamed of us, he presents us in God's presence as his brothers. The meaning of the second quotation (Is. 8:17) is not clear. Perhaps the author wanted to remind us of the trust in God which Jesus displayed on the cross, as an example to those Christians who were in danger of wavering in their faith because of the trials and sufferings they were forced to endure.

Man's Destiny is to Die; God's Son Takes This on Himself (2:14–15)

[14]*As these children all share flesh and blood, he too shared likewise in them, so that by his death he might bring to nothing him who has power over death, that is, the devil.* [15]*So he would free those who were held in bondage by the fear of death all their life long.*

Flesh and blood are the characteristic marks of our earthly existence; they are death's peculiar sphere of influence. The Epistle to the Hebrews regards death as an unnatural event which is contrary to God's plan; it is proof that the world is subject to the devil. The inevitability of death gives rise to fear and makes it impossible for man to feel really free. It has been pointed out quite correctly that this description of our human situation is in keeping with an existentialist view of the world. But there is another common attitude towards death which consists in taking life and death as they come, the flippant renunciation of any effort to decide our future destiny. A purely formal faith in the world to come is particularly exposed to this danger.

Our High Priest is Faithful and Compassionate; He Atones for Sin and Helps Those who are Tempted (2:16–18)

[16]*He does not take the angels' part; he takes the part of Abraham's offspring.* [17]*Consequently, it was fitting that he should become like his brothers in every respect, so that he might be a compassionate and faithful high priest in what concerned God, to atone for the sins of the people.* [18]*In that he has suffered, as one who was tempted himself, he can now come to the aid of those who are tempted.*

Here we come to the pith of the argument. In God's Son, who assumed flesh and blood and became like us in every respect, we have been given a high priest on whose compassion and fidelity we can rely. He has suffered (something of which we are afraid); he was tempted (and withstood the temptation— something we cannot always be sure of in our own case). He

has power to help us where no one else can help us—in the
loneliness of sin and death. And there is something else we must
not forget: Temptation in the biblical sense arises not only
from the attraction of what is forbidden, but also when a man
is overcome with discouragement and the oppressive sensation
of complete futility—which is often worse.

*Look at Jesus, the Faithful Apostle and High Priest Who, as God's
Son, is Head of his Household (3:1-6)*

¹*Then, holy brothers, companions of a heavenly calling, consider
the apostle and high priest of the faith we profess, Jesus, ²who
is so faithful to him who made him, just as Moses was in his
[God's] house. ³For greater honor was paid to him than to
Moses, just as greater honor is enjoyed by the man who built a
house than by the house itself. ⁴Every house is built by someone,
but it is God who has made everything. ⁵And Moses [was]
certainly faithful in his [God's] whole house as a servant, bearing witness to what was to be spoken. ⁶But Christ [was faithful]
as a Son over his [God's] house. We are his house, if we keep
[firm to the end] our confidence and the hope which is our
boast.*

The Christological theme of the letter is developed, not for its
own sake, but to hold up an example before the eyes of the
faithful who had grown tired. They must learn to consider
Jesus and so acquire a share in him (cf. 3:14) or, as it is put
in this section, they must become God's house. " God's house "
was one of the titles of honor enjoyed by the Israelites as the
liturgical community of the Old Testament. They are in the

house who remain faithful to their heavenly calling, with the fidelity Christ himself showed towards God. The author goes into some detail concerning the fidelity shown by " Jesus the high priest and apostle." To it he devotes a scriptural proof which we can no longer follow in all its steps. This can be explained only in the light of the situation in which the Christians to whom the letter is addressed found themselves. Their loyalty was beginning to waver; some already avoided the liturgical assembly (cf. 10:25). Complete apostasy from the faith would only be a short step. Moreover, we must not forget that such apostasy can occur in many ways. It need not necessarily mean an open break with the community; inner obstinacy may be enough, a course of conduct which is unworthy of a calling which comes from heaven and leads to heaven.

Do Not Harden Your Hearts against God's Call and His Promise (3:7—4:13)

A Quotation from Psalm 95: 7–11 (3:7–11)

[7]*Therefore, as the Holy Spirit says: " Today, if you hear his voice,* [8]*do not harden your hearts as when you were embittered in the time of temptation in the wilderness;* [9]*for your fathers tried [me] in the test, and [yet] they saw all I had done* [10]*for forty years. So I became angry with that generation and said: They always go astray in [their] hearts. They do not recognize my ways,* [11]*so that I swore in my anger: They will never enter my place of rest."*

The text which the epistle takes as the basis for its message of

warning, which is also—as we shall soon see—a message of
promise, is inspired by the Holy Spirit. The Holy Spirit must
also make the meaning of his words clear to us and soften the
hardness of our hearts.

The wanderings of the chosen people through the desert into
the promised land, God's place of rest, seem to have become a
favorite theme of Christian preaching at a very early stage.
When the Corinthians displayed a weakness for impurity and
idolatry, St. Paul reminded them of the terrifying example of
the desert generation (1 Cor. 10: 1–13). However, while the
Apostle of the Gentiles refers immediately to the pentateuch
account, the Epistle to the Hebrews chooses the second part of
Psalm 95 as the basis for its homily. This choice is important
as the psalm gives the general impression of being a processional
hymn which was used in the liturgy to summon its hearers to
make their way into the sanctuary: " Come, let us rejoice in the
Lord. Let us exult in the rock of our salvation. We must come
before his face with thanksgiving and cry jubilantly before him
with hymns of praise! . . . Enter! Let us fall down and bow
low, kneeling before the Lord who made us " (Ps. 95: 1–2.6).
At first sight, it might seem extraordinary that this solemn,
joyous invitation to join in the liturgy should be associated with
the memory of the tribulations and the wanderings of the desert
period. But, in reality, the two ideas are not so different as they
might seem. The liturgical approach to God's presence is merely
a symbol of what happens on the level of ordinary life. Whether
or not a man will really enter God's place of rest depends, not
on his liturgical behavior, but on his obedience towards God in
the trials of everyday life.

The Septuagint version of the Bible which the epistle follows
here as in all other quotations translates the Hebrew place names

" Meriba " and " Massa " into Greek according to their etymological sense. In this way, " Embitterment " and " Trial " (in the sense of putting God to the test) become stopping places on the journey through the desert which makes up our human life.

A Warning against Disbelief and Sin (3: 12–14)

¹²*See to it, brothers, that there may not be in any of you an evil heart filled with disbelief, and prepared to fall away from the living God.* ¹³*Instead, you must encourage one another, day after day, as long as this " today " is proclaimed, so that none of you may be hardened by sin's treachery.* ¹⁴*For we have been made companions of Christ, provided that we hold fast to our first confidence to the end.*

The author addresses the whole community and not, as we might expect, only those Christians who were in danger of losing their faith. As brothers, we all have an obligation to watch over one another and especially to care for those who no longer listen to God's voice. Such pastoral responsibility is not confined to " superiors " (13:17) only; every Christian is called upon to keep his eyes open and prevent his brother from being lost. What we today would call the " priestly " power of exhortation or *paraklesis* has been given to everyone. A word of encouragement or warning may counter the " sclerosis " of the heart, that spiritual hardening which makes a man bitter, dissatisfied, and selfish. Anyone who allows himself to be deceived by sin ends by severing his bond with the living God. He renounces his share in Christ and cuts himself off from the community of salvation, the assembly of those who are called to God's heavenly rest. Increasing loneliness and isolation are the lot of those who do not hold fast to the confidence which faith gave them at the beginning.

This Warning is Meant Only for the Disobedient (3:15—4:2)

¹⁵*When we read: " Today, if you hear his voice, do not harden your hearts as when you were embittered . . ."* ¹⁶*who were the listeners, who were those who were " embittered "? Were they not all those who were led out of Egypt by Moses?* ¹⁷*With whom was God angry for forty years? Was it not with those who had sinned, whose bodies littered the desert?* ¹⁸*To whom did he swear that they would not enter his place of rest, if not to those who were disobedient?* ¹⁹*And so we see that they could not enter, because of their disbelief.* ⁴:¹*We must be afraid, then, lest any of you should seem to have failed; the promise of entry into his place of rest still stands.* ²*The good news was proclaimed to us, as it was to them. Yet the message to them did them no good, because it was not fused by faith into a unity with those who heard it.*

God took an oath that the Israelites who left Egypt would not enter his place of rest, the promised land. The Epistle to the Hebrews could have chosen simply to base the teaching it gives the Christian church on this event, as it is described in scripture. However, for our author, scripture is not merely something which concerns the past and is addressed to those who lived in the past; it is an appeal addressed directly to us today. Consequently, the use he makes of this text in his homily is far more than a mere moral application of the story; on the contrary, he wants to impress on his readers and hearers the relevance here and now of what the Holy Spirit said in times gone by. If, then, the threat contained in Psalm 95 is still valid, what basis can Christians have for their hope of being able to enter God's resting place?

First of all, the author makes it clear that God's anger was directed only at those who had sinned, those who would not obey and refused to believe. From this it follows that the way to God's rest still remains open for those who have faith. For them, the warning message is a message which brings good news. We are the pilgrim people of God; we are constantly exposed to the temptation to quarrel with God and lose sight of the promised land, making light of God's will. True faith, on the other hand, proves itself by obedience and unshakable fidelity to God's word. God's word must almost enter into a chemical union with us; otherwise, it will be no more use to us than it was to the Israelites in Moses' day.

God's Rest and His Six Days' Work (4: 3–5)

[3]*Because we have faith, therefore, we enter the place of rest, as God said: " Then I took an oath in my anger: They shall not enter my place of rest," although his works have been finished since the foundation of the world. [4]Yet one passage says concerning the seventh day: " God rested on the seventh day from all his works " (Gen. 2:2). [5]But here we read again: " They shall not enter my place of rest."*

In the context of Psalm 95, the term *rest (katapausis)* evokes the idea of the land of Canaan. It was there that the Israelites who had wandered about the desert with no permanent dwelling place had finally settled down; it was there that they were to enjoy peace and security from their enemies. The God of the covenant who had accompanied his people on their journey through the desert was no longer forced to dwell in a tent; the temple became his " place of rest " on earth (cf. Is. 66:1; Ps. 131:14; Acts 7:49). It was natural for the Epistle to the Hebrews to transpose this Old Testament idea to the heavenly world to come. Christians have been promised a new and supernatural Canaan where they will find rest at last from all the distress and anxieties of life.

The section we are dealing with now introduces an additional idea, namely, the idea of God's rest on the seventh day of creation. When the six days were over, God rested from all his works; in the same way, the faithful will one day be able to rest from their work (cf. Rev. 14:13). However, the text involves more than a simple comparison. The emphasis is on the identity of the " rest " God enjoyed after the creation and the rest to which the pilgrim people of God is called. What the epistle has in mind, obviously, is not a share in some divine attribute or state; on the contrary, it is the same heavenly reality which is described in other passages as " the world to come," " the true sanctuary," " the heavenly country," and " the lasting city." God's place of rest is thought of as a country which has been ready since the beginning of the world. We meet the word " rest " almost exclusively in the liturgy of the dead; we associate it with the idea of an intermediate state proper to a soul separated from the body (or even to the body reposing in a tomb). Consequently, it may seem strange to us when our final salvation in Christ is described as a form of " rest." But if we remember how our lives are filled with raucous unrest, haste, and activity, so that we can never really rest, we too will come to look forward to the heavenly *katapausis* as a " consummation devoutly to be wished."

A Final Exhortation (4: 6–11)

⁶*Since, then, it remains true that some enter this place of rest, and those who were given the good news in the first place do not enter because of their disobedience,* ⁷*God once more appoints a day, " today," announcing it, when a long time had passed, through David, as has already been said: " Today, if you hear his voice, do not harden your hearts."* ⁸*If Jesus (that is, Joshua) had led them into this rest, God would not have spoken about another day afterwards.* ⁹*Therefore, a sabbath of rest still awaits the People of God.* ¹⁰*For the man who has entered his rest has rested from his works, just as God, too, rested from his.* ¹¹*We must strive eagerly then to enter that rest, so that no one may fall and become an example of disobedience like them.*

In conclusion, the homily once more sums up the principal themes and issues an urgent warning against disobedience. It was this refusal to obey which prevented the Israelites in the wilderness from entering God's rest. Moreover, the conquest of Palestine under Joshua did not bring them to their promised goal either. To prove his contention, which seems self-evident to us, the author cites an argument we often meet in St. Paul (for example, Gal. 3:17). The words of Psalm 95 were first spoken a long time after the conquest; therefore, they must refer to some other event, to a new " today." On the level of scientific exegesis, this proof may be quite untenable, but the author's general intention deserves to be noted. It is a fact that, in its Christian interpretation, the Old Testament does not recount past events; on the contrary, it explains our own future to us, so that we may pass the test here and now, " today." The Epistle to the Hebrews, therefore, shows us how we must listen to the Old Testament as a message which affects our own lives and forces us to come to a decision.

A Hymn to the Word of God Which Has Power over Life and Death (4:12–13)

[12]*God's word is something living; it is charged with power, sharper than any two-edged sword. It penetrates to the division of soul and spirit, of joint and marrow. It judges the feelings and desires of our hearts.* [13]*No creature is hidden from it. Everything is naked and exposed before its gaze—and we must render our account to it.*

This hymn comes at the end of the first part of the letter; it takes our minds back to the beginning. In former times, God spoke through the prophets; now he has spoken through his Son. No one can afford to ignore his word simply because it seems to be merely another word which involves no deeds. It is true that the world cannot complain of being short of words, above all of words that are beautiful, good, noble, and sublime. Has God, then, nothing more to offer than his word? Of course, God has done more than " simply " speak; in his Son's death, he also let us hear his silence—but this silence " speaks louder than Abel's blood " (12:24). Once more, therefore, we are reduced to what is, humanly speaking, a weak and helpless word. It is only by faith that we can see the power and the life which are enshrined in God's word. God's word has power to decide the world's fate. We may turn a deaf ear to it and ignore it innumerable times; we may consciously throw it to the winds and behave in a way which defies it, but one day the moment of truth will come for all men. God's despised and humiliated word will one day demand an account.

JESUS' HIGH PRIESTHOOD (4:14—10:31)

The long center section of the letter is enclosed between two
" brackets " (4:14–16 and 10:19–31) which have essentially the same
content. They give us an idea of what the author is trying to bring
home to us in his presentation of his subject, which is very difficult
at times. We have " a great high priest who has passed through the
heavens " (4:14) and opened a way for us to the true holy of holies
by his blood (10:19–21). Realizing this, we must now "hold fast
(to the hope) we profess " (4:14; 10:23) and "approach the throne
of grace with confidence " (4:16; cf. 10:22). The point in both
passages, therefore, is once more steadfastness and loyalty in the
faith. This faith must find joyful expression in the liturgical assembly
(10:25), as well as in fraternal exhortations to mutual love and good
works (10:24).

Jesus, our High Priest, the Son of God (4:14—5:10)

We Have a High Priest who Can Sympathize with Us (4:14—5:3)

¹⁴*Now that we have a great high priest who has passed through
heaven, Jesus the Son of God, we must hold fast by what we
profess.* ¹⁵*The high priest we have is not one who is incapable
of sympathizing with our weaknesses; on the contrary, he was
tempted like us in every way, except that he is without sin.*
¹⁶*Now we must approach the throne of grace with confidence,
so that we may find mercy and grace to help us in our time of
need.* ⁵:¹*For every high priest is taken from among men and*

appointed for men in what belongs to God, to bring gifts and sacrifices for sins. [2]He is able to sympathize with those who are ignorant and go astray, because he too is hemmed round by weakness. [3]Therefore, he must offer sacrifices for his own sins as well as for those of the people.

The Epistle to the Hebrews is not composed like a scientific essay which deals with one thought after another in a strictly logical order. Rather, it resembles a symphony in which various themes and motifs are skillfully blended with one another. The theme of the compassionate high priest, for example, has already been touched upon briefly (2:17), but then it receded into the background once more. In this passage, it appears again, and now it will be treated in detail as the first reason on which the exhortatory part of the long middle section of the letter is based. We must hold fast by what we profess and approach the throne of grace confidently, that is, without fear and in the certainty of being heard—because, despite his heavenly dignity, our high priest has a heart which can feel for us.

It has frequently been remarked that the author of the Epistle to the Hebrews lacks the warm intimacy with Christ which characterized the apostle St. Paul to such a marked degree. The portrait of Christ which we find in the epistle is like an ikon; it is a solemn, liturgical image; it seems to be inspired more by biblical speculation than by a vivid experience of the faith. It is true that such remarks are well-founded, and we shall have occasion to confirm them repeatedly. However, the author himself probably felt this lack and tried to compensate for it by emphasizing Christ's compassionate mercy very strongly. St. Paul experienced the redeeming love of the Son of God in concrete fashion on the road to Damascus. The author of the Epistle to the Hebrews, on the other hand, was dependent on tradition for his knowledge of Christ, and he had to confirm it with proofs based on scripture or reason. As a result, it may be that his descriptions at times appear rather academic; it is up to us to make them come alive. We can never be sure how our fellow human beings judge our faults, whether they condemn and reject us out of hand, or overlook everything in complete indifference. But we know the attitude Jesus adopts towards sin; and we also know that he never refuses to help a sinner who turns to him for help.

Our High Priest Received His Vocation from God and Owes His Appointment to Him (5:4–10)

⁴And no one takes such an honor for himself, unless he is called by God, like Aaron. ⁵Christ, too, did not claim the glory of being a high priest for himself. It was God who addressed him: " You are my Son. I begot you today " (Ps. 2:7). ⁶In the same way, he says in another passage: " You [are] a priest of the order of Melchizedek for ever " (Ps. 110:4). ⁷In the days of his existence in the flesh, Jesus offered prayer and entreaty to God who had power to save him from death, with a loud cry and tears. And he was heard because of his reverence. ⁸Although he was the Son, he learned obedience from what he suffered, ⁹and now that he has reached his goal, he has become the author of eternal salvation for all those who are obedient to him. ¹⁰He was addressed by God as a " high priest of the order of Melchizedek."

The Old Testament contains numerous accounts of people who were divinely called, but not one of them was called to the priesthood. In Israel, a man was a priest by birth, because he was descended from one of the families which had served in this ministry from the earliest times. Naturally, people believed that the ancestors of these families had been appointed to this office by God. However, even in Aaron's case, there is nothing to show that he was called directly by God (Ex. 28:1). With the prophets, things were different. God's word was addressed to them without warning and found them unprepared. He summoned them to his service, when, where, and as he pleased. Why is it, then, that the author of the Epistle to the Hebrews does not refer to Moses, Isaiah, Jeremiah, or Ezekiel? The various accounts of how they were called occupy a prominent place in the Old Testament. Instead, he refers to Aaron, who was a rather colorless figure. The explanation is easy. " Christ " (The " Anointed ") was appointed to his heavenly office the way priests were appointed, not after the manner of the prophets. We could say that he " inherited " (cf. 1:4.5) this office from God who begot him as his Son.

Despite this, however, the psychological or, if we prefer, the charismatic element was not wanting in Jesus' vocation to the high priesthood. God's Son was obliged to become, in the days of his existence in the flesh, what he already was from all eternity. According to the synoptic tradition, Jesus used the word " Abba " to address God in the garden of Gethsemane and gave himself up to his Father's will as his Son. This scene is taken here as a symbol of his whole life on earth. Here, too, there is a reference to the situation of the church of the time. The " loud cry and tears " refer to the fear and despair Christians felt at the thought of the bloody persecution to come, rather than to the passion as it is described in the gospels. The epistle wants to make it clear to these Christians and to us that only obedience and reverence (cf. 12:28) will open the way to our heavenly consummation. But if the Greek term *eulabeia* ("religious fear") was to be translated "fear," as it is in many commentaries, the verses would be more difficult. We should have to say that God "hears" us, that is, that he frees us "from fear," but that he does not save us from a bitter death.

A Digression:
The State of the Community (5:11—6:20)

The Recipients of the Epistle are Like Children (5:11–14)

[11]*We have to speak at length about this and it is hard to speak intelligibly, because you have become so hard of hearing.* [12]*By this time, you should be teachers yourselves. Yet you need to be taught once more, and taught the rudiments of God's words. You are like those who must be fed on milk, not on solid food.* [13]*Anyone who takes milk is ignorant of the holy teaching; he is only a child.* [14]*Adults, on the other hand, need solid nourishment, those who have accustomed their minds by practice to distinguish between good and evil.*

Jesus is a priest of the order of Melchizedek. Before explaining the meaning of this mysterious title to his readers, the author interposes a fairly long exhortation. This is aimed at arousing their curiosity and explaining his purpose. To what extent the first readers of the epistle were themselves prepared for its involved thought processes is one of the unsolved mysteries of the exegesis of this letter. The common opinion is that the author wanted to communicate the fruits of his own scriptural expertise to them. If this is correct, it made it even more necessary that he should excite their interest and make them realize how much depended on their careful attention. However, there is no doubt that the recipients of the letter were more familiar with many of its concepts, images, and ideas than we are. The author's exegetical procedure probably did not seem so strange to them as it does to us. Above all, they knew the literal text of the " profession of faith " which the epistle clearly sets out to interpret.

More important than the possibility of understanding the epistle on an intellectual level is the religious and moral problem of the willingness to understand it. This involves readiness to listen to the message of scripture and accept it. The author has not much to say in his readers' favor, in this respect. Their conversion and baptism were already far behind them; yet, no one could say they had reached maturity as Christians. Indeed, it would really have been necessary to begin from the beginning once more and teach these Christians the first elements of their faith all over again. They needed to be fed on milk, not solid food. As is clear from other passages of the New Testament (1 Cor. 3:1–2; 1 Pet. 2:2), the epistle here employs a figure of speech which was common in antiquity and is quite comprehensible in itself. Difficulties arise only when we try to explain what is " milk " and what is " solid food " in a Christian context. It is precisely the truths which seem most simple and fundamental that often involve the greatest difficulties. Moreover, if readiness to accept the message of scripture is lacking, because a person has become " hard of hearing," even infants' food would not be much use.

A Beginner's Catechism and a Word for the Initiates (6:1–3)

¹*Therefore, we must leave aside the introductory teaching about Christ. We will devote ourselves to the completion, and not start at the beginning again, talking about conversion from lifeless deeds and faith in God, ²with instruction about baptism, the laying on of hands, the resurrection of the dead, and the eternal judgment. ³We will do this, if God permits it.*

The author enumerates the subjects about which he is not going to speak in great detail. On the other hand, he describes the subject of his discourse in the single word *teleiotes*, which is not easy to translate. It probably means what concerns the " completion." This refers to a more advanced knowledge of the doctrine of salvation as only a mature Christian could grasp it, in contrast to the fundamental Christian catechesis. The chapters which follow give us a sufficient indication of what the epistle means by a doctrine intended for " those who have been completed " or initiated.

At this point we must devote a little more attention to the introductory teaching. The care with which the author enumerates these points is not unpremeditated. When a speaker introduces a number of points which he wants to impress particularly on his hearers by saying that he does not intend to discuss them, he is merely employing a well-known rhetorical device. The fact is that the rudiments of Christianity which are mentioned here must form the basis of all further developments in theological speculation. The renunciation of " lifeless deeds " (cf. 9: 14), faith in God (11: 6), and the eternal judgment (9:27; 10:27.30; 12:23.25.29), are subjects which the author can never leave out of his sight. The distinction he makes, therefore, is not really an objective, systematic division of the material; its significance is mostly rhetorical and psychological. He does not want to treat his readers like neophytes, like unbaptized pagans, although this is really what their religious and moral situation calls for. When he describes his letter as an instruction for those who have been completed or initiated, it is meant to arouse their legitimate Christian ambition. In reality, he can never do more than develop and deepen the introductory instruction they have already received. It would be wrong to imagine that a man must first renounce " lifeless deeds " and believe in God, and then make a further decision in virtue of which he accepts the gospel message concerning Christ. The epistle counters this misunderstanding by describing the introductory teaching explicitly as a " message concerning Christ."

A Warning Against Irreparable Apostasy (6:4-8)

⁴[It is] impossible that those who have been enlightened once and for all and have tasted the heavenly gift and been given a share in the Holy Spirit, ⁵and experienced God's good word and the powers of the aeon to come, ⁶and have then fallen away, should be brought back once more to repentance. They crucify the Son of God, to their [own condemnation], and expose him to contempt. ⁷The ground which drinks in the rain which falls so abundantly, and bears a crop which is useful to those for whose sake it was tilled, receives a blessing from God. ⁸But if it produces only thorns and thistles, [it is] useless and near to being cursed. Its end is the fire.

This grave warning can be interpreted correctly only if we

remember its literary form. It is the word of a pastor of souls who is anxious to ward off the danger of imminent apostasy by enlarging on its frightful consequences. It is not the decision of a moralist or canonist concerning the question whether lapsed Christians who were truly sorry for their sins could be taken back into the community of the church; this question became acute in the second century. In other words, the author does not mean that a second conversion is impossible; he merely wants to summon his readers to a change of heart and to reflection, while there is still time. The enumeration of the saving blessings conferred in baptism is clearly meant to be a pressing appeal. The man who is preparing to reject the faith and abandon the Christian community should remember the miraculous manifestations of the Spirit in former years. As long as the break with Christ has not been made definitive, there is a possibility that such favors may be experienced again.

Good and bad Christians are now contrasted with one another in a short but very effective simile. Good Christians are like the Garden of Eden which flowed with the blessings of heavenly grace; they prove themselves members of the community, and they are assured of an eternal reward. The others are like the earth which was cursed after the fall. They are a scandal and a disappointment to their fellow men, and they run the risk of being destroyed in the flames of a terrible judgment at the end.

There is Good Hope of Improvement (6:9–12)

⁹*But where you are concerned, dearly beloved, we are convinced things will turn out for the best and bring you to salvation, even while we speak to you as we do.* ¹⁰*God is not unjust; he will not*

forget your activity and the love you have shown for his name by serving the saints and continuing to serve them. ¹¹However, it is our ardent wish that each of you should give proof of the same eagerness to the end, with your eyes fixed on the full assurance of your hope. ¹²You must not become lazy; on the contrary, you must imitate those who inherit the promises by their faith and patience.

Encouraging those who have become faint-hearted and are in danger is one of the most important tasks of a pastor. Like Jesus, he must be careful not to " snap the reed that is already crushed, or extinguish the wick that still glimmers " (Mt. 12:20). Even the harshest warnings spring from a love which is determined to seek out those who are lost and bring them home. The author of the Epistle to the Hebrews has often been accused of inclining to exaggerated strictness. It has been said that he is a rigorist who has failed to preserve the spirit of the gospel in all its purity. Such criticisms could be justified, if individual expressions are taken as they stand and raised to the level of dogma. But if we remember the author's pastoral intention, we see that he could scarcely have spoken otherwise than he did. His pessimistic and gloomy view of the fate of those who have fallen away from the faith is coupled with an even greater degree of optimism concerning the salvation of those who hold fast to Christ with perhaps one last despairing effort. What is the reason for his confidence? His surest guarantee is the divine justice; God will let no good deed go unrewarded.

We ourselves may forget our own past and feel no inclination to recall the degree of self-sacrifice and love for our neighbor of which we were once capable. But it is all recorded in God's unfailing memory. It is self-evident that this truth must not be abused as an excuse for subsequent negligence. A Christian cannot put his hands in his pockets and appeal to the enthusiasm he once showed, to justify himself. The whole point is that we must revive an era when love, the proof of our active faith, was still alive in us.

The epistle now addresses its exhortations to the community as a whole, and not to individual Christians. Praiseworthy examples of enthusiasm and effective love are still to be found in the community, beside the regrettable signs of a falling off in fervor. This, too, gives the author confidence that his wish that all Christians may once more live an exemplary Christian life will not go unfulfilled. The one thing all the members of the community stand in need of is patience inspired by faith which waits without doubting for the promise to be fulfilled.

Abraham and the Divinely Guaranteed Promise (6 : 13–20)

13When God gave Abraham the promise, he swore by himself because he had no one greater to swear by: 14" Truly will I bless you with blessings; I will make you increase and multiply" (Gen. 22 : 17). *15And so, after great perseverance, Abraham attained the promise. 16Men, for their part, swear by something greater than they, which serves to confirm their oath and so put an end to all contradiction. 17Similarly, when God determined to give the heirs of the promise abundant proof of the irrevocable character of his decision, he gave them a guarantee by an oath. 18Because of these two inalterable facts, in which God could not have deceived us, we are greatly encouraged, as we take refuge in them, to hold fast to the hope which awaits us. 19This hope is an anchor for our souls, a firm anchor which reaches in behind*

the veil [20]*where Jesus has already gone in before us, a high
priest of the order of Melchizedek for all eternity.*

The exhortation returns gradually to the theme of the Melchizedek priesthood of Jesus. Once more it is clear beyond all
possibility of misunderstanding that the epistle is not interested
in theological speculation for its own sake or as a means of
satisfying the intellectual curiosity of its readers. The deeper
knowledge of Christ and his saving activity serves to confirm
Christians in their faith and hope (love will be discussed again
in Hebrews 10:24). The principal reason for the various signs
of weakness and falling off in fervor in the community was the
fact that the second coming of Christ which had been promised
had not yet taken place. The Christians who were tired of
waiting are reminded of the example of Abraham. Two ideas
which have a further role to play in the later development of
the letter cut across one another in the course of this proof:
God's promise is infallible in itself, but he confirms it with a
solemn oath; Abraham inherited the promise only after a long
and patient wait. The idea of God swearing an oath (the
" second inalterable fact," v. 18) may seem strange and anthro-
pomorphic to us, but great importance was attributed to it in
the contemporary philosophy of religion. Basically it is merely
a symbol of the inviolable and definitive character of God's
promise, and one that is easily understood. As we shall soon
see, Jesus too was appointed God's high priest with an oath
(7:20-21).

The idea of patience inspired by faith, and perseverance in
adverse circumstances, occurs once again in the third part of the
letter (10:36; 11:13.39; 12:1). In the present passage, the author
is more concerned with the fact that our hope of salvation as

Christians already has one foot firmly planted in the heavenly world. As the nautical and liturgical language of the passage puts it, this hope is " like an anchor . . . which reaches in behind the veil." In practice, this means that as our precursor and high priest, Jesus has already reached the goal towards which we are all journeying. The chapters which follow will tell us why and in what way this has come about.

Jesus' Melchizedekian Priesthood (7:1–28)

Melchizedek the Priest-King (7 : 1–3)

¹*This Melchizedek was the king of Salem and a priest of the most high God. He went out to meet Abraham, as he returned from the victory over the kings, and he blessed him.* ²*Abraham also gave him a tenth of everything. His name is first interpreted as " King of Justice " and then also as King of Salem, that is, " King of Peace."* ³*There is no mention of his father or mother; there is no family tree; there is no mention of the beginning of his days or the end of his life. Instead he is like the Son of God. He remains a priest eternally.*

In Genesis 14:7–20 we read: " As Abraham was returning from his victory over Chedor-laomer and the kings who were allied with him, the king of Sodom went out to meet him in the Valley of Shaveh (that is, the Valley of the Kings). But Melchizedek produced bread and wine; he was a priest of the most high God. And he blessed him, saying: ' Abraham is blessed by the most high God, the Creator of heaven and earth. Praised be the most high God who has given you all your enemies into

your hands.' And Abraham gave him a tenth of everything."
Apart from Psalm 110:4, this is the only passage of the Old
Testament in which we hear of Melchizedek. Christian writers
subsequently came to regard the offering of bread and wine
made by the priest-king of Jerusalem as a prophetic allusion to
the Eucharist.

The interpretation of this incident given in the Epistle to the
Hebrews, however, follows a different line and regards the
mysterious figure of Melchizedek as a type of Christ, the Son
of God and the eternal high priest. We have here a particularly
clear example of the extraordinary exegetical methods favored
by the author. Genesis mentions the king of Jerusalem, who
was also a priest of El Elion, the supreme deity of the Canaanites,
without saying anything about his ancestry or his subsequent
history. From this our author concludes that Melchizedek had
no father or mother, that he was not born, and that he did not
die. Many other persons who are mentioned only in passing in
the Old Testament could be regarded as prototypes of the eternal
Son of God with equal justification. That our author chose
Melchizedek rather than anyone else is explained by his priestly
office and by the fact that Abraham acknowledged him as his
superior, when he gave him a tithe of his spoils. The author of
the Epistle to the Hebrews was probably not the first to suspect
some ontological mystery in connection with the priest-king of
Jerusalem; the qualification " without a father and without a
mother " could scarcely be the result of genuinely Christian
speculation.

Jesus is the Son of God, because God is his Father in a way
which is entirely unique. However, this truth is not stressed
particularly in the Epistle to the Hebrews. The Father-Son
relationship is mentioned only by implication in the quotations

from Psalm 2 : 7 and 2 Samuel 7 : 14 (cf. Heb. 1 : 5). God is never referred to as the " Father " of Jesus Christ, as is so often the case in St. Paul and St. John (cf. however, Heb. 12 : 9: "The Father of the spirits "). It is possible, therefore, that the author bases his speculation on a somewhat different conception of Jesus' divine Sonship. However this may be, the important thing is Jesus' person as he was in himself, not the categories and examples used by the author which were determined by religious and historical factors. We must try to see him in all the personages and events of the Old Testament. Modern exegetical methods, however, adopt a more sober and objective approach.

Melchizedek is Greater than Abraham or Levi (7 : 4–10)

⁴See, then, what a great figure this man is. Even the patriarch Abraham gave him a tenth of his first spoils. ⁵Those of Levi's sons who have received the priesthood are commanded to take tithes from the people according to the law, that is, from their own brothers who are also descended from Abraham. ⁶But this man is not one of their descendants; yet, he took tithes from Abraham and bestowed a blessing on the bearer of the promises. ⁷Without fear of contradiction, we can say that it is always the person who is lower that is blessed by one who is higher. ⁸In this case, too, it is mortal men who accept the tithes. In the other case, however, it is one who we are told lives on. ⁹We can even say that, in Abraham, Levi had to pay tithes himself, although he exacts tithes from others. ¹⁰He was present in the patriarch's loins when Melchizedek went to meet him.

It would be easy to conclude from these verses that the author was intent on belittling two of the most important representatives of the Jewish faith, Abraham and Levi. In point of fact, it was believed for a long time that the readers of the letter were Jewish Christians who were tempted to return to their old faith and worship. According to this opinion, the author had to convince them of the superiority of the Christian priesthood of Melchizedek over levitical worship, to prevent them from relapsing into Judaism. This solution may appear very suggestive, but it is quite unacceptable. The exhortatory (parenetic) section of the letter never attacks Jewish institutions; on the contrary, its whole purpose is to summon its readers to a living faith in Christ and warn them against falling away from the faith completely. A second and equally important point is that the author, as a Christian writer, starts exclusively from realities which are described in the Old Testament. At the time when he wrote, the temple of Jerusalem had already been in ruins for several years; the role of the Jewish priesthood was at an end. All that remained was God's word. There a Christian theologian could see that in former times levitical priests existed whose ancestor Abraham had been blessed by a greater priest. The new Melchizedekian priesthood of Jesus, with whom alone this epistle is concerned, is older and more exalted than the priesthood of the Old Testament which originated from Levi. Even Abraham paid homage to this eternal priesthood by paying tithes.

The Priesthood and the Law (7 : 11–19)

¹¹*If the levitical priesthood had brought completion—and it was with this in view that the law was given to the people—would there have been any need to appoint another priest of the order*

of Melchizedek, not of the order of Aaron? ¹²*If the priesthood is changed, there must of necessity be a change in the law too.* ¹³*The person of whom this is said (that is, that he belonged to the order of Melchizedek) came from a different tribe, none of whose members was entitled to approach the altar.* ¹⁴[*It is*] *clear that our Lord arose from the tribe of Judah, and Moses said nothing about priests from this tribe.* ¹⁵*This is even more clear, when another priest is appointed after the model of Melchizedek* ¹⁶*who became a priest, not according to the law of a norm based on the flesh, but by the power of unending life.* ¹⁷*Our Lord is given this testimony: " You are a priest for ever, of the order of Melchizedek "* (Ps. 110:4). ¹⁸*Now, of course, the former rule is being abolished because of its insufficiency and uselessness—* ¹⁹*the law did not bring completion—but a better hope is substituted* [*for it*], *by means of which we draw near to God.*

It is the task of the priesthood to bring men to completion. The word *teleiosis* is not easy to translate; our epistle takes it to mean eternal salvation and entry into God's place of rest in the world to come, the heavenly sanctuary. When a man has attained his goal by the mediation of the priesthood, he is " completed." This also means that he is perfect in the moral sense; his sins have been forgiven and God has sanctified him, consecrating him for his service. All these various nuances are implied in this word. In many passages of the Old Testament, the word is also used to mean " priestly consecration " (Lev. 8:33; 2 Mac. 2:9). However, neither the levitical priesthood nor the Mosaic law which was associated with it was capable of bringing completion.

For this reason, it was necessary to institute another priesthood which was independent of the genealogical qualifications im-

posed by the Mosaic law. This meant striking a blow at the
heart of the law; the law had proved itself powerless and in-
effective. Significantly, however, the epistle does not speak of a
new law; instead, it substitutes for a norm " based on the flesh "
the " power of an unending life " and " a better hope by means
of which we draw near to God." These two phrases enshrine the
essence of the Christian economy of salvation and worship. This
is concerned with the conquest of death and sin, the hostile
forces which prevent us from having free access to God. We
could say that the gift of " the power of an unending life " and
the ability " to draw near to God " really constitute the essence
of the completion which the old law and the levitical priesthood
tried in vain to impart.

The Guarantee of a Better Covenant (7 : 20–25)

²⁰[This, too,] did not [take place] without an oath, although
those others became priests without any oath. ²¹Jesus [became a
priest] with an oath sworn by him who said to him: " The
Lord has taken an oath and he will not repent: You are a priest
for ever" (Ps. 110:4). ²²To this extent, therefore, Jesus has
become the guarantee of a better covenant. ²³Those others became priests in great numbers because death prevented them
from continuing in office. ²⁴Jesus, however, because he remains
for ever, exercises the priesthood without end. ²⁵Therefore he
can also save for ever those who approach God through him; he
lives on constantly to intercede for them.

The taking of an oath by God has already been mentioned in
connection with the promise made to Abraham (cf. 6:13–17). In

this passage, the author cites Psalm 110 which confirms Jesus' Melchizedekian priesthood with a divine oath. As we have seen, a divine oath is a figure of speech which is intended to emphasize the inviolability and the definitive character of God's word. But, then, what about God's word when it is not confirmed by an oath? Must we make a distinction in the case of God's word as we do with human assertions, where we distinguish between ordinary human words which may conceal falsehood or deceit and a solemn oath upon the truth of which we can rely unconditionally? Obviously, this cannot be. However, his theory of a divine oath compels the author to suppose that a certain classification exists in the Old Testament. There are assertions, as, for example, the promise made to Abraham, which demand our unconditional assent independently of any oath (cf. 6: 17–18). On the other hand, the author clearly does not regard the law " proclaimed by angels " (2:2) as coming directly from God; it is only a provisional, " fleshly " arrangement which is incapable of bringing " completion." For the same reasons, the levitical priesthood which was instituted without an oath could not be regarded as an unchanging and eternal institution of divine origin.

The covenant which the levitical priesthood served with its sacrifice had to be replaced by a " better " covenant with Jesus for its guarantee; his priesthood was confirmed by a divine oath. Here for the first time we meet the word covenant (*diatheke*) which appears as a key-word in the following chapters. First, however, the author develops an idea with which we are already familiar, the life and death contrast which exists between the two priestly orders. The levitical priests were mortal men; consequently, there had to be a great number of them to provide for the temple ministry at any given time and also in succession to one another. Jesus enjoys the power of an unending life (7:16), and he remains the only priest in his order for all eternity. The salvation he wins for those who approach God through him shares the same qualities as his priesthood; it is unique and definitive. It can never be surpassed. The letter speaks of "saving," to show that it is not for us to choose whether we wish to turn to God or not. We are forced to seek God's favor by the fear of death which threatens our existence from the very first moment (2:15; 5:7) and by the despair which grips our conscience as we struggle in vain to be free of the burden of our sins (9:9; 10:1–3).

A Hymn of Praise to the Heavenly High Priest (7 : 26–28)

26*This was the kind of high priest we needed, holy, and free from all stain of evil. He is set apart from sinners and raised higher than heaven.* 27*He has no need each day, like the other high priests, to make an offering for his own sins first, before offering for those of the people. He accomplished this once and for all when he offered himself.* 28*The law, on the other hand, appoints men who are loaded with weakness. The word of the oath which [came] after the law [appointed] the Son who has been completed for ever.*

Chapter 7 ends with what we could describe almost as a hymn of praise in honor of Jesus the high priest. Anyone might feel inclined to wonder and ask why sinful and mortal men like ourselves "needed" a high priest who is so holy and so exalted above everything earthly. The epistle obviously does not mean that we have any claim to such a high priest, or that it would be beneath our dignity to be led by a high priest who was just as sinful and mortal as we are. The fact is, we " needed " a heavenly high priest because no other priest could have helped us. Only Jesus, who took the part of sinners without becoming a sinner himself, and overcame death by being exalted at God's right hand, had power to save us. These verses, then, bring to a close the author's discussion of Jesus, the high priest of the order of Melchizedek, and summarize the conclusion which flows from the contrast between God's oath and the law. At the same time, they introduce the important chapters which follow, which deal with the offering the heavenly high priest made of himself.

Priest and Mediator of a New Covenant (8:1—10:18)

A Priest in the Heavenly Sanctuary (8 : 1–5)

¹*This is the chief point of what has been said: We have such a person as our high priest; he has taken his place at the right hand of the throne of majesty in the heavens. ²He is the minister of the sanctuary and the true tent of meeting which was erected by the Lord, not by man. ³Every high priest is appointed to offer gifts and sacrifices. Therefore our high priest, too, had to have something to offer. ⁴But if he was still on earth, he would not be a priest at all, because there are already priests to offer gifts according to the law. ⁵They are ministers of something which is only a copy and a shadow of the heavenly [realities]. When Moses was preparing to construct the tent, he was told: " Be careful. You must make everything according to the model which was shown to you on the mountain " (Ex. 25: 40).*

The theme of the letter now nears its climax, its " chief point."
We are finally about to learn where and how Jesus exercises his
ministry as a high priest of the order of Melchizedek. It will
come as a surprise to hear that he exercises his office as high
priest in heaven, and not on earth. He ministers in a sanctuary
which was created directly by God. This is the only genuine,
true, and real sanctuary. Jesus could not have ministered as a
priest on earth because there the gifts and sacrifices to be offered
are prescribed by the law. We already know (Heb. 7:27) that
the heavenly high priest has offered himself, once and for all.
However, before taking this decisive point as its central theme,
the epistle first sets the stage. This gives us an idea of the entire
cosmic and eschatological significance of the events on Golgotha.

The author and very probably his readers also were familiar
with the idea of a sanctuary in heaven which is found in the
Old Testament and the apocalyptic literature. It is doubtful,
however, whether the passage cited here (Ex. 25:40) originally
meant anything more than that Moses constructed the tent of
meeting according to a heavenly model or plan. On the other
hand, the Book of Wisdom, which is one of the more recent
books of the Old Testament, unmistakably refers to the temple
at Jerusalem as a " copy of the holy tent which you prepared
from the beginning " (Wis. 9:8). Many apocalyptic writers
boasted that they had seen the heavenly sanctuary. " The angel
opened the gate of heaven for me. I saw the holy temple and
the glory of the Most High on the throne " (*Test. Levi* 5; cf.
Rev. 4:1–11). The rabbis even believed that the heavenly sanctuary was exactly opposite the earthly one, and that the worship
offered by the angels above corresponded with that of the priests
below, even in the smallest details. It is possible that the author
of the Epistle to the Hebrews adopted these ideas, but in his

explanation of the heavenly sanctuary and of the sacrifice of atonement which is offered in it he follows a path of his own. The most we can conclude from the present passage is that Jesus is the high priest of the true, real, and genuine sanctuary, while the levitical priests minister in a sanctuary which is only a copy and a shadow. God himself established the sanctuary; the tent of meeting was the work of men. This distinction clearly betrays a Platonist attitude which measures earthly realities by the heavenly reality which is their prototype. However, it is certain that the Epistle to the Hebrews is not merely preaching philosophy; on the contrary, it is intent on explaining the meaning of Christ's death which has transformed heaven and earth, with the help of Alexandrine learning.

Mediator of a Better Covenant (8 : 6–13)

⁶*But now he has received a superior ministry, just as he is the mediator of a better covenant which was established on better promises. ⁷If the first [covenant] had been blameless, no room would have been sought for a second one. ⁸But God finds fault with it, saying: " See, the days are coming, says the Lord, when I will make a new covenant with the house of Israel and the house of Judah. ⁹It will not be like the covenant I made with their fathers on the day when I took them by the hand to lead them out of the land of Egypt. They did not remain steadfast in my covenant and I paid no more attention to them, says the Lord. ¹⁰This [is] the covenant which I will make with the house of Israel after those days, says the Lord. I will implant my laws in their minds and inscribe them on their hearts. I will be their God and they will be my people. ¹¹No longer will each man*

have to instruct his fellow citizens, or a brother his brother,
saying: Recognize the Lord! For they will all know me, from
the least to the greatest of all. ¹²*I will have mercy on their*
iniquities and remember their sins no more " (Jer. 31:31–34).
¹³*In speaking of a " new covenant," God has abolished the first*
covenant as antiquated. What has grown old and is out of date
is on the point of disappearing.

If Jesus is a priest in the heavenly sanctuary of which the earthly
sanctuary is only a figure, his ministry must be far superior to
and more effective than the worship of the Old Testament, with
its efforts to placate God by gifts and sacrifices. This superiority
becomes particularly clear if we compare the promises of the Old
Testament with those of the New Testament, of which Jesus
is the mediator. At first sight, it might seem as if the letter was
wandering away from the point, as if the institution of a new
covenant had nothing to do with Jesus' priestly ministry. However, we have only to think of the story of the Last Supper, with
which our author was certainly familiar, to realize that this is
wrong. There the connection between Jesus' death on the cross
and the institution of the new covenant is stated explicitly.
The role played by the priests of the Old Testament in the conclusion of the various covenants mentioned in the Bible may be
less clear. But when we view the matter in the light of Christ's
action we see that a priest's ministry consists in establishing
the covenant with God and constantly renewing it; he must
bring it to its final achievement. It was the task of the heavenly
high priest to accomplish the promises which constitute the
essence of the new covenant and make them a reality, so that
they were no longer merely something that was preached. The
priestly ministry, therefore, is in the service of God's promises,

a thought which we also meet in St. Paul in a different context (Rom. 15:8).

The long quotation from Jeremiah mentions four of the blessings which are promised. The last of these, the forgiveness of sins, is the most important for the train of thought in our epistle (cf. 9:14–15.22.28; 10:3–4.12.17.18). However, we must not overlook the other promises made for the new covenant; the law written in or on our hearts, the divine community of the people of God, and the instinctive and universal knowledge of God. When a covenant was made in the ancient East, the text of the agreement, the law of the covenant, was inscribed on stone tables which were then preserved in the sanctuary (cf. 9:4). This was what happened at Mount Sinai. But now God writes the " law " of the new covenant in our hearts, so that we know ourselves what we have to do. In this way, the new covenant as it is written in our hearts and minds appears as the positive side of the forgiveness of sins (cf. 10:16-18).

The second great blessing which is promised is the eschatological communion of the people with their God. This, too, only seems to take second place to the forgiveness of sins. It is true that the quotation: " I will be their God and they will be my people " does not occur again in the epistle, but the idea of an eschatological community of worship can be said, without exaggeration, to be the basic theme of our letter. On the other hand, the promise of an instinctive and universal knowledge of God plays no further part in the author's reasoning. Yet, he was familiar with spiritual experiences (6:4–5); baptism meant for him: " Receiving the knowledge of the truth " (10:26). Indeed, by this time, his readers should have been in a position to instruct themselves and others (5:12). However, he certainly does not share the optimism of the First Epistle of St. John, according to which Christians " have no need to be taught by anyone," because " they are instructed about everything by the Spirit " (1 Jn. 2:20.27).

The Earthly Sanctuary (9 : 1–5)

¹It is true that the first [covenant], too, had its rules for worship and the earthly sanctuary. ²For a tent was prepared, the first, in which were the lamps and the table, and the loaves laid out. This was called the " holy place." ³But behind the second curtain was the " holy of holies" as it was called. ⁴This contained a golden incense altar and the ark of the covenant, which was covered with gold on all sides. In this were a golden jar with the manna, Aaron's staff which sprouted, and the tables of the law. ⁵Over it were the cherubs of glory, overshadowing the throne of mercy. We are not going to speak about these in detail now.

Moses had the tent of meeting constructed according to the pattern of the model which was revealed to him on the mountain (8:5). If, therefore, we want to know what the heavenly sanctuary where Christ acts as our high priest is like, we must look at the tent of the old covenant. The most important thing about it is that it was divided into two parts. It consisted of a first or outside tent, the " holy place," and the holy of holies which was hidden behind a curtain. The epistle lays such emphasis on the separation between the holy place and the holy of holies that we could easily get the impression that two different tents were involved. In the philosophical and religious world of the Epistle to the Hebrews, the allegorical interpretation of the tent of meeting was nothing unusual. The Hellenistic

Jewish historian, Flavius Josephus, regarded the two parts of the tent as a figure of the entire universe with the division between heaven and earth (*Ant.* 3.6.4). Philo of Alexandria explains that the first or outside tent represents the world of the senses, while the holy of holies stands for the world of spiritual and eternal ideas.

The description given in our letter also conceals a deeper meaning. The holy place contains only simple things, such as are used every day—lamps, a table, and the presentation bread. The holy of holies, on the other hand, enshrines only very costly and sacred things, all of which glitter with gold. To emphasize this, the author places the golden incense altar in the holy of holies, although its place was outside the curtain according to Exodus 40:26 (cf., however, 40:5). For the same reason he fails to mention that the lamps were of pure gold and that the table was plated with it. This gives us some idea of the symbolic meaning the author gives to the tent of meeting with its two sections. The first tent, the holy place, is a symbol of the earth, a place in which we move every day. The holy of holies, then, must be an image of heaven, God's gracious presence. Despite all the gold and glory of its furnishings, the second tent still belongs to the " cosmic " sanctuary; in other words, it is still inextricably involved in a world that is figurative, shadowy, and provisional.

The Priestly Ministry in the Earthly Tent (9: 6–10)

⁶*As it was arranged like this, priests go into the first tent at any time, to perform their acts of worship.* ⁷*But into the second tent only the high priest once a year, and not without a blood offering which he makes for himself and for the sins of ignorance com-*

mitted by the people. ⁸This is an indication from the Holy Spirit that the way to the sanctuary was not yet revealed, as long as the first tent continued to exist. ⁹This is a symbol of the present time, in accordance with which gifts and offerings are presented which are unable to bring the worshipper to completion where conscience is concerned. ¹⁰They deal only with kinds of food and drink, with various ablutions and other rules of the flesh, which remain in force only until the time of the true dispensation.

The division of the tent of meeting into two parts was also responsible for a twofold division in the type of ministry performed by the priests of the Old Testament. The priests could enter the first tent at any time, but the second tent, the holy of holies, could be entered only once a year by the high priest on the great Day of Atonement. Even he could enter only after he had offered a sacrifice of blood for sin. The blood of the animal which was slaughtered was sprinkled on the mercy-seat, the throne of the divinity, in the holy of holies. We cannot say with certainty whether the brief phrase " not without an offering of blood " refers to the sacrifice offered for sin or to the ceremony in the holy of holies. The epistle probably only means to say in general that an offering of blood to atone for sin is absolutely necessary for entry into the holy of holies. The emphasis is on entrance into the holy of holies, while the numerous other complicated rites of Leviticus chapter 16 are not mentioned. This results in a profound change in the meaning of the great Day of Atonement. The Old Testament rite of atonement has become an eschatological mystery of worship. The all-important thing now is to find the " way into the sanctuary," and enter God's holy of holies, the place where our salvation is completed.

The Old Testament could not fulfill this hope. It only gives a mysterious indication from the Holy Spirit that the way to the heavenly sanctuary would not be opened as long as the first tent continued in existence and was valid. What does this cryptic statement mean? The first tent, the " holy place " or the tent of meeting as it is called, is not merely an antechamber to the holy of holies; it also stands for the whole earthly order of worship in the Old Testament which is based on the flesh. As long as the gifts and sacrifices prescribed by the law were being offered, there was no way into the heavenly holy of holies. of allusions. As we shall soon see in greater details, our concerned "; in other words, there was no real forgiveness of sins. Over and above this, however, the first tent also has a more comprehensive significance. It stands for the earth, in contrast to the holy of holies which is a symbol of heaven. Therefore, the " way into the (heavenly) sanctuary " can be opened once and for all only when the material creation has given way to the new world which is to come.

Finally, the opposing concepts flesh and conscience have an important role to play in this difficult passage which is so full of allusions. As we shall soon see in greater detail, our conscience can attain its rest only in God's true holy of holies; that is its real home. The " flesh," on the contrary, is explicitly referred to as the first tent and the rules it imposes which are wholly concerned with prescriptions concerning food and various ablutions. Therefore, we will not be introducing a foreign element into the text, if we connect the " continued existence " of the first tent with the continued existence of our earthly bodies. For those who serve God, the " way to the sanctuary " is opened only when the earthly tent of their mortal bodies is destroyed. This interpretation presupposes, of course, that

the way through the curtain has already been inaugurated
(cf. 10:20) and that the " time of the true dispensation " has
already begun.

Christ's Priestly Ministry in Heaven (9 : 11–14)

¹¹*But Christ has come as the high priest of the true blessings,
by means of the greater and more perfect tent which was not
made by hands, that is, which does not belong to this creation.*
¹²*By his own blood, not by the blood of goats and calves, he
enters once and for all into the sanctuary, having found eternal
redemption.* ¹³*If the blood of goats and calves and the ashes of a
cow, when they are sprinkled, can sanctify those who have
incurred some stain, with a purity belonging to the flesh,* ¹⁴*how
much more will not Christ's blood purify our conscience from
lifeless deeds, so that we can serve the living God; he offered
himself through the eternal Spirit, as an immaculate offering to
God.*

The author now begins his description of the counterpart to the
Old Testament rite of worship which was based on the " flesh."
In the person of Christ, the priesthood and the law are changed
completely (7:12). It is only to be expected that the scene of his
priestly ministry should be different from the very beginning.

A historian would say that Jesus lived on earth, that he died
on the cross, and that he was then taken up into heaven, as his
followers believe. If we take this factual outline to be the basis
of the Epistle to the Hebrews, we must conclude that it con-
siders Jesus' death on the cross as an event which took place
outside the heavenly sanctuary. Its sole purpose, then, would be

to provide the blood which is necessary to enter heaven. In point of fact, many commentators hold that Christ became a priest only in heaven, where he presents the blood he shed on the cross before God. Such an interpretation does justice neither to the importance of Christ's death nor to the line of argument followed in the epistle. Let us recall briefly what has already been said about Jesus' priestly ministry: Our high priest has passed through heaven (4:14); he has offered himself once and for all (7:27); he has taken his place at the right of the throne of majesty (8:1); he is a minister of the sanctuary and of the true tent established by God, and not by men (8:2); he could not have been a priest on earth (8:4). There are also other passages which sound as if Jesus received his appointment as high priest for the first time in heaven (5:10; 6:20). On the other hand, the figurative explanation of the atonement ritual of Leviticus 16 can only mean that, when Jesus offered himself on the cross, he did so as a high priest and so passed through heaven to God's throne. The idea that Jesus' passion and death were not a sacerdotal offering is absurd. It is refuted in several ways in later statements (9:26.28; 10:5-14).

The present passage also makes it clear that Jesus has already " come," " appeared," or " made his debut," as our high priest. The author is obviously not speaking only of the ascension; he is giving a theological interpretation of Jesus' entire life. Unlike the external rites of the old covenant, Jesus' priesthood confers blessings which are " real " (cf. 10:1). We can be sure this refers to the " better " promises of the New Testament (8:6), the forgiveness of sins and final union with God. Jesus can procure these blessings for us, because of the superiority of the priestly ministry he exercises. His ministry is not confined to the realm of the earthly tent which is only a shadow; it is exercised in the

" greater and more complete tent which was not made with hands and does not belong to this creation." The application of the ritual framework of Leviticus 16 to the person of Jesus and his ministry leads to almost insoluble difficulties of interpretation. In that passage, we are told how the high priest passed through the outer tent before entering the holy of holies, and it is this thought which is emphasized in the passages which follow (9:24; 10:12.20). But what does the author mean by the tent which belongs to the heavenly sanctuary, through which Christ our high priest had to pass? We must be careful here to separate the image from the reality, as in a parable. The metaphorical idea of a space which we get from Leviticus 16 does not have to have any parallel in the case of Christ, in the form of some region which is sacred. Therefore, it is certainly wrong to start thinking about the " lower regions of heaven " or any other " suprasensible region." The daring figure of a " tent which was not made with hands and does not belong to this creation," which seems so strange to us, is intended to be a theological description of Christ's entire historical existence. The earthly, outer, tent of the old covenant could never have done this; it could never have served as a basis for our entry into the true holy of holies in heaven, but this has now been done by the " greater and more complete tent," Jesus' life.

Even Christ could not enter the holy of holies " without blood " (9:7). But his sacrificial death resulted in an eternal atonement; he has power to purify men from all their sins, past, present, and future. There can be no doubt that Christ's blood has cleansed our conscience from all the lifeless works we committed before our baptism. It is not quite clear from the present passage whether or not the epistle is also thinking of the forgiveness of those sins which a Christian is conscious of and which affect his ability to join in the common worship. However, we must be careful not to separate the two points of view too much. The certainty that baptism marks a new beginning, and that a Christian is now capable of serving the living God, also gives us the assurance that Christ's blood has the power to cleanse us of the guilt we incur by our " lifeless works " day after day. The phrase recalls the prescription of the Old Testament according to which contact with a corpse made a person ritually unclean (Num. 19:11–22). We ourselves are the corpse by whose contact we are made unclean.

The Testator's Death (9:15–17)

¹⁵*He is the mediator of a new* diatheke *[testament or covenant], so that after the death occurred which was to atone for the transgressions committed under the first covenant, those who were called should receive the promise of an eternal inheritance.* ¹⁶*Where there is a* diatheke, *the testator's death must follow.* ¹⁷*A* diatheke *becomes legally effective only in case of death; it produces no effect as long as the testator is still alive.*

The author changes his images and comparisons in rapid succession. While the image of the great Day of Atonement is still before our eyes, the epistle suddenly switches once more to the idea of the new covenant. But then the train of thought is interrupted by a juridical consideration. The word *diatheke* in Greek can mean either the covenant as a religious institution, or an ordinary testament. The author skillfully avails of this double meaning to prove that the new covenant only became effective through Christ's death. The heir succeeds to an inheritance only after the person who made the testament has died. In the same way Christ, too, had to die before we could enter into the enjoyment of his promised inheritance.

This line of argument seems obvious, and yet a number of questions remain which force us to reflect. Christ is first of all described as the " mediator " of the new covenant, but in the juridical reasoning he appears as the testator who made the testament. There is no mention of God in this connection; yet the proof would only be conclusive if we were told that God died, so that we might inherit his promises. We are inclined to reject the idea that God could die as absurd. But is not this precisely what we call the absurdity, the folly, of the cross? Why did God become man, if not " to destroy, by his death, the one who had power over death " (2 : 14), that is, the devil? The usual distinction that Jesus died as man, not as the Son of God, is not enough. In any event, our epistle teaches that the Jesus who died was the one who had himself made God's great testament.

Moreover, the testator's death is clearly portrayed as having a lasting effect and lasting validity. It was not merely a transient event which was cancelled by Easter. On the contrary, the whole theology of the epistle aims at presenting Christ's sacrificial death on the cross as an event which remains for ever as a never failing source of salvation.

The Blood of the Covenant (9 : 18–22)

[18]*For the same reason, the first covenant, too, was inaugurated with blood.* [19]*When all the commandments of the law had been proclaimed before the people by Moses, he took the blood of calves and goats with water and sprinkled the book and the*

whole people with crimson wool and hyssop, ²⁰*saying: " This is*
the blood of the covenant which God has established for you "
(Ex. 24:8). ²¹*He also sprinkled the tent and all the liturgical*
furnishings with blood in the same way. ²²[*The fact is*] *that*
almost everything must be purified with blood according to the
law; there is no remission [*of sin*] *without the shedding of*
blood.

The section devoted to the law of succession is only a link in a
longer chain of proof. The author wants to show his readers or
listeners that the new covenant, with the better promises it
makes, could only come into force with Christ's death. To us this
seems quite unnecessary; we are inclined to regard Jesus' death
on the cross as something to be taken for granted. But could
God not have forgiven us our sins without the sacrifice of his
Son? Why did blood have to be shed? Even if the Old Testament was forced to demand a blood ritual as a means of atonement, surely God's gracious word would have been enough in
the new covenant: " Go in peace! Your sins are forgiven you! "
Moreover, we see that in New Testament times there was a
widespread dislike of blood sacrifices, which resulted in what we
would call a " spiritualization of the idea of worship." The
sacrifice of animals was taboo in Egypt particularly, where the
author of our letter probably received his intellectual formation.
By means of the allegorical interpretation of Scripture, the Jews
of Alexandria tried to find a spiritual meaning underlying the
Old Testament prescriptions concerning such rites. It is possible
that the readers of the Epistle to the Hebrews felt a similar
dislike for blood offerings. We do not know.

It is scarcely possible now to reconstruct the psychological outlook presupposed by the letter. The important thing is, how-

ever, that we ourselves should have a better understanding of the
necessity of Jesus' death. Here the Old Testament idea of the
institution of the covenant on Mount Sinai can be very helpful.
It is noteworthy that the author describes the Old Testament
events in some detail; on the other hand, he is very sparing in
his application of them to the new covenant, and he quickly
returns to the idea of the great Day of Atonement. Are we to
suppose, as is often the case even with accomplished speakers,
that our author had not complete control of all his thoughts and
associations of ideas? That he tries to follow various lines of
thought which are suddenly torn from his grasp, or turned in
other directions? His description of the liturgy which took place
on Mount Sinai contains the remarkable addition not found in
the Exodus account (Ex. 24:3–8) that "even the book" was
sprinkled with blood. We are certainly entitled to ask, is there
not here some relevant Christian meaning which is hidden? The
author may have wanted to imply that the gospel message must
be understood in the light of the cross, and that no promise is
worth anything unless it is written in blood. It is with this in
mind that we must then consider whether Jesus' death on the
cross may not have been an inevitable consequence of his proclamation of God's forgiving grace. In that case, his violent death
would not have been an isolated or chance happening; it would
not be a meaningless event, but the inevitable outcome of his
preaching. However this may be, we cannot be content with
conventional answers, when it comes to having a true grasp of
Jesus' death, and this also holds for the answer given in this
epistle.

It is noteworthy that the epistle speaks of the blood of the
Sinaitic covenant in a formula which is an obvious reminiscence
of the words of our Lord at the Last Supper (Mk. 14:24). Yet,

the connection with the eucharistic celebration is not explicitly stated either in this or in any other passage. However, this does not mean that we are forbidden to think of the Lord's Supper in which the blood of the covenant which was shed for the remission of sins is acclaimed and shared by the participants.

A Unique and Better Sacrifice (9 : 23–28)

²³If it is necessary to purify what is only a copy [of the realities found] in heaven by means of such [rites], the heavenly [realities] themselves will need greater sacrifices still. ²⁴For it is not into a sanctuary made with hands that Christ has entered, an image of the true sanctuary; he has entered heaven itself, to appear now before God's face for us. ²⁵Nor did he enter, to offer himself repeatedly, as the high priest enters the sanctuary year after year by means of blood which is not his own; ²⁶otherwise he would have had to suffer repeatedly since the beginning of the world. But he has appeared only once at the end of the ages, to do away with sin by his sacrifice. ²⁷It is laid down for man that he must die once and after that the judgment; ²⁸similarly Christ, now that he has been sacrificed once to do away with a great many sins, will appear a second time without sin, for the salvation of those who wait for him.

All the authors of the New Testament believe that, by God's providence, there is a strict correspondence between the old and the new covenant. They realized, of course, that the Old Testament prophecies were fulfilled in Christ in a way which was at once better and more perfect than any which the prophets could have imagined. In many instances, it must also have been very different from what they expected. However, the author of the Epistle to the Hebrews was the only one who conceived the correspondence between the old and the new covenant in what amounts to a philosophical formula. The Alexandrine idea of the heavenly or typical world and the earthly world which is only a copy made it possible for him to describe exactly the essence and the " place " of the revelation which was made in Christ. The events, blessings, and institutions of the new covenant belong to the world of " heavenly " realities, and they need a " better " sacrifice to purify them. Under the influence of the Old Testament forerunners of Christ's sacrifice, the author uses the plural of the noun here. However, there can be no doubt that he is thinking of Christ's one and only sacrifice on the cross. This blood offering has opened the way to God's true holy of holies; it has purified the heavenly realities, the place and the objects used in the worship of the New Testament. In other words, it has made them capable of honoring God really and truly (cf. 9 : 14). We must never forget that, for the Epistle to the Hebrews, the heavenly realities are not some far off, apocalyptic region; on the contrary, they are things which affect us directly, for example, our conscience which can be cleansed from sin only by Christ's blood. This is the way St. John Chrysostom interprets the reference to the cleansing of the heavenly realities, which seems so strange to us at first: " What does he mean by heavenly realities? Heaven, or the angels perhaps? He is not referring to any of these. What he means is what belongs to us " (PG 63 : 125).

One of the essential characteristics of the heavenly and typical world is the fact that the event which gave rise to it occurs only once. In the realm of earthly realities, on the other hand, which are only a reflection of the heavenly world, the same processes must be gone through again and again. The significance of the " once and for all " character of all that concerns Christ and his community of salvation will be discussed in greater detail in chapter 10. Here we should like merely to draw attention to a sentence which sounds like a platitude, but which has a more profound meaning in the present context: " It is laid down for man that he must die once, and after that the judgment . . ." (v. 27). The assertion that we must all die once is nothing new; but the realization that our death shares the definitive and once-and-for-all character of Christ's sacrifice of atonement on the cross should make us think. The parallel which exists between our death and Christ's death on a purely formal level can and should lead to an objective similarity of content. If that is so, we have no need to be afraid of the judgment, unlike those who have rejected Christ's cross (cf. 10:26–31).

The Shadow and the Archetype (10:1–4)

¹The law contains only a shadow of the blessings to come, not the archetype of these things itself [and can, therefore,] never bring to completion for all time those who approach with the same sacrifices year after year. ²Otherwise these sacrifices would surely have ceased, because the worshippers would have had no consciousness of sin any more, once they had been purified. ³On the contrary, by means of them [the sacrifices] the memory of sin [was recalled] year after year. ⁴It is impossible that the blood of bulls and goats should take away sins.

The law and the gospel are related to one another as the shadows and the archetype of the blessings of salvation, the world of divine realities. A similar comparison is found in Colossians

2:17. There, however, the distinction is between the " shadow of the (things) to come " and " Christ's body." The basis of this comparison, therefore, is the simple image of a physical body which casts its shadow before it. In the Epistle to the Hebrews, on the other hand, we have a threefold division, " shadow," " archetype " (*Eikon*), and " things," a division which is also found in Philo of Alexandria. This Jewish philosopher and religious thinker thought that the " eikon " stood between God and the visible world; it was at once God's image and the archetype of the material universe. Therefore, it was identical with the Logos and the invisible spiritual world of ideas. Once more, the author of the Epistle to the Hebrews avails of this Platonic outline to emphasize the essential difference between the Christ-event and the Mosaic law. The Christ-event does not belong to the shadowy dispensation of the old covenant which was only a copy (cf. 8:5); it is the visible revelation of the heavenly world of the divine archetypes. The sacrifices prescribed by the law were merely shadowy anticipations of the saving blessings Christ brought; as such they could not achieve their purpose and do away with sins for ever. The mere fact that these rites had to be repeated proves their lack of success. If they had been conscious of being cleansed from the state of sin once and for all, the worshippers of the Old Testament would have stopped offering these sacrifices.

It is clear that this line of argument is conclusive only on the supposition that the atoning sacrifices of the Old Testament were intended to achieve a reconciliation which would be perfect and final. If we consider the question from a historical viewpoint, however, we see that the goal which the levitical worship set for itself was far more modest. The fact is that it was concerned only with an atonement which was limited in its scope, both temporarily and with regard to the objects affected. The hope of a redemption from sin which would be accomplished once and for all and remain valid for ever is found for the first time in the context of the Jews' eschatological expectations. Christ's followers believed that he had appeared " at the end of the aeons " (9:26), to save the world; his death on the cross, therefore, must have really taken away the sins of the world once and for all. By the time the Epistle to the Hebrews was written, a difficult problem had already arisen. How was it that many Christians could still commit sin, and even fall away from the faith, if final redemption had really taken place? Added to this was the delay in Christ's parousia which prolonged the dangerous circumstances Christians lived in. It is easy to see that doubts about the efficacy of Christ's sacrifice of atonement were bound to arise. Perhaps, after all, his blood did not have power to purify us from sin once and for all. This also helps us to see why the author of the Epistle to the Hebrews was not content merely with the traditional eschatological argument to prove the atoning power of Christ's death; instead, he bases his proof principally on the heavenly character of Christ's sacrifice which is the archetype of all other sacrifices. This Alexandrine approach did not depend on the time of Christ's second coming. Even if his parousia was still further delayed, it would make no difference to the once-and-for-all effect of Christ's death which is valid eternally.

The Offering of Christ's Body (10: 5–10)

⁵*Consequently, as he enters the world, he says: " You did not want a sacrifice or offering, but you prepared a body for me.* ⁶*You did not wish for holocausts and sin-offerings. ⁷Then I*

said: See, I am coming—as it is written about me in the book—
to do your will, O God" (Ps. 40: 7–9). ⁸First he says: " You did
not want sacrifices or offerings, holocausts or sin-offerings; you
did not wish for them." Yet these were offered in obedience to the
law. ⁹After that he said: " See, I am coming to do your will." He
takes away what was first, to establish what is second. ¹⁰It is in
this [God's] will that we are made holy by the offering of the
body of Jesus Christ, once and for all.

Previous passages speak only of blood, but here Christ's body,
too, is mentioned as the sacrificial victim. It is true that the
choice of the word " body " was prompted by the quotation
from the psalm (Ps. 40: 7–9), but we are perfectly entitled to ask
whether the author may not have chosen this psalm precisely
because it mentions a body. The word " body " must have reminded Christian listeners immediately of the Eucharist. Here
again, it is remarkable that the author does not make the
obvious reference to the Lord's Supper explicit. To us his silence
seems strange, but one reason for it was that, in New Testament
times, the Eucharist was never treated more or less as an isolated
reality, as it often was in later sacramental piety. As St. Paul
tells us, the Lord's Supper heralded the " Lord's death " (1 Cor.
11 : 26); in other words, it reminded Christians of the atoning
and saving efficacy of Christ's cross. The Epistle to the Hebrews
pursues a similar aim; the author is intent on convincing the
faithful of the purifying and sanctifying efficacy of Christ's
sacrifice which brings us to completion. Obviously, he does not
do this in the same way as the liturgical commemoration of
Jesus' death; he acts as a theologian and a pastor who must
create the spiritual and moral conditions which will enable his
community to approach the altar of grace " with true hearts and

in the full certainty of the faith " (10:22; cf. 4:16). To this extent we can say that the homiletic section of the epistle is a " mystagogical discourse "; it gives its readers an insight into the celebration of the Eucharist by deepening their faith in the atoning power of Christ's death and explaining its theological basis.

The passage we are dealing with now contains a scriptural proof which is intended to show that the " offering of the body of Jesus Christ " was in fulfillment of a divine decree which existed from all eternity. God did not want the sacrifices prescribed by the law; it was Christ's offering of himself which revealed for the first time where God's preference really lay. The attitude which the epistle adopts towards the Old Testament here seems contradictory. On the one hand, scripture is regarded as a direct revelation of God's will; it contains the script of the heavenly drama of salvation. In the psalm, the eternal Son speaks to God on his entry into the world, to give an authentic explanation of the meaning of his life, passion, and death. On the other hand, the epistle will not admit that the sacrifices which the Old Testament regarded as having been instituted in accordance with a divine command were really an expression of what God wanted and intended. The criticism which the prophets directed against certain forms of worship from time to time is regarded as a rejection and condemnation of the entire levitical form of worship in principle. Within the Old Testament, therefore, there are two orders or spheres which are referred to respectively as the " first " and the " second." It is clear that this description is intended to remind us of the distinction between the first and second tent and the first and second covenant. By his entry into the world at the Incarnation, Jesus abolished the first tent, the sphere of earthly rites based on the " flesh." In its place, he established the second or the heavenly tent in which he makes an offering of the body which was prepared for him by God personally. Here once more, Christ's Incarnation and his passion, the cradle and the cross, are viewed as a single whole. This confirms what we have already said: That the Epistle to the Hebrews regards Jesus' whole life on earth as a single sacrifice which leads through the " greater and more perfect tent " to God's holy of holies. " See, I am coming to do your will."

Christ's Sacrifice is Final and Cannot be Repeated (10:11–18)

¹¹Every priest continues to minister day by day, offering the same sacrifice repeatedly, a sacrifice which can never take away sins. ¹²But Jesus offered only one sacrifice for sins [and then] took a place at God's right hand for all eternity, ¹³waiting now until his enemies are laid as a footstool for his feet. ¹⁴For by means of one offering he brought to completion for all time those who were to be made holy. ¹⁵The holy Spirit, too, testifies to this. For after he has said: ¹⁶" This is the covenant I will make with them after those days, says the Lord. I will put my laws in their hearts, and inscribe them in their minds," he adds: ¹⁷" I will not remember their sins or their iniquities any more" (Jer. 31:33). ¹⁸Now where forgiveness of these sins [is granted], [there is] no more sacrifice for sin.

The author is in a hurry to bring his discussion of Jesus' ministry as our high priest to an end. The whole point of his letter becomes increasingly clear. By the sacrifice of his death on the cross, Jesus won final salvation for himself and for his followers. He himself has reached his goal in heaven where he now shares God's throne. He has nothing to do now but wait peacefully until " his enemies are laid as a footstool for his feet," as the author says in a quotation from Psalm 110:1. The Epistle to the Hebrews obviously does not attach so much importance to the dramatic events of the end of time on which the apocalyptic writers concentrated all their attention. The decisive eschatological event has already taken place; the faithful can now look forward calmly to what is still to come. They, too, have been brought to " completion "; the way to God's holy of holies is open for them. It is true that they have not yet taken their place in heaven, like Christ; they are still on the way and there is a danger that they may fall back into disbelief and sin. To ward off this danger, the epistle tries to make its readers, who are hesitant and weary, realize that Christ has already done everything for them. But if they reject the forgiveness that has been offered them and cancel it, they must be aware that there is no other means of wiping out the guilt of their sins.

An Exhortation and a Warning (10:19-31)

Let us Approach (10:19-22)

[19]*Brothers, we now have the right to enter the sanctuary, thanks to Jesus' blood.* [20]*He dedicated it for us as a newly opened and living way through the curtain, that is, his flesh.* [21]*We also [have] a great priest who is over God's household.* [22]*Let us then approach with a true heart in the full certainty of the faith, our hearts cleansed from a bad conscience, our bodies washed in clean water.*

" Let us approach "—we have already heard this invitation to a

procession before (4 : 16). But now we know why the way to the
" throne of grace " is open. Jesus' blood, that is, his bloody death
on the cross, has given us the " *parrhesia* " we need to enter.
This word can only be translated imperfectly in English. In the
first place, it means a right, an authorization, to enter the heavenly holy of holies. But it also means the subjective attitude of
joyful confidence inspired by the realization that Jesus' blood has
enabled us to draw near to God at any time. The background of
the great Day of Atonement is once more extended to become a
symbol of our entire human life. We are all on the way—where?
On earth, our road is a road of death; it leads only as far as the
dark curtain, the insurmountable wall of our prison which is
watched over by diabolical powers (cf. 2 : 14–15). Is there something, then, on the other side, behind the curtain? A holy of
holies planned and executed by mere human beings, a world of
ideologies and wishful dreams? At the most, such a sanctuary
would be only a copy of the heavenly realities, a negative fore-
taste of God's true sanctuary which has been revealed to the
world in Jesus Christ. It is here that the people, God's family,
find for the first time the new way to heaven which they have
not yet trodden. This is the processional route which has been
consecrated by Jesus' blood; it leads to the living God and to life.

But this road, too, has its curtain of death which separates
what is provisional from what is final. This curtain is Jesus'
flesh which was sacrificed on the cross. In the earthly tent, the
curtain prevented access to the holy of holies; it was a barrier
which could not be surmounted. Jesus' flesh, on the other hand,
is a curtain which gives the faithful access to God at all times.
Once more, the thought of the eucharistic liturgy is very close;
there the community eat Jesus' flesh and drink his blood " to find
mercy and grace at the throne of grace, to help them in their

needs " (4 : 16). On what other occasion could this " approach "
take place in the church? The least we must say is that every
other approach to God, in personal prayer, in the practice of
charity, or finally in death, receives its meaning from the celebration of Jesus' death in the Eucharist.

We also have other grounds for approaching God's presence
with joyful confidence. We have a great high priest who is over
God's household. In this brief formula, the epistle sums up all
that it has already said in previous chapters about the compassionate, loyal, and sympathetic help the heavenly high priest has
for his church, when it is tempted and endangered. The
" approach " the faithful make to the sanctuary is paralleled by
Jesus' " intercession " before God as their high priest and the
mediator of the covenant (cf. 7 : 25). This is the reason why the
conditions imposed by the epistle for such an approach—a true
heart, the full certainty of the faith, the purification of our bad
conscience, and bodily purity—also appear as the result and the
consequence of this approach. The epistle is certainly thinking
primarily of baptism and its purifying effect. However, the
church actualizes the state it acquired in baptism by the approach
which it makes in the liturgical celebration. In this way, it once
more becomes conscious of the forgiveness which it has received
once and for all and rejoices over it. In these verses, the Epistle
to the Hebrews gives us the first principles on the basis of which
we may conclude that a Christian can repent at any time; by
God's grace, which is always ready to forgive, he can overcome
his daily failings and sins. Unfortunately, this implication of the
text is often overlooked. The distinction between such " venial "
(that is " forgivable ") sins and " mortal sins " which are " unforgivable " in principle is not the same as in later moral
theology, but this should not surprise us.

We Must Hold Fast by What We Profess (10 : 23–25)

²³*Let us hold fast by the profession which gives us hope without wavering, for he who has given us a promise is faithful.* ²⁴*We must watch one another, to incite one another to charity and good works.* ²⁵*We must not forsake our own assembly, as* [*is*] *the custom with some; on the contrary, we should encourage one another, and this all the more as you see the day drawing near.*

We have already heard the exhortation to hold fast by what we profess, in a previous passage (4:14). Now, however, we have a better idea of the content of this profession. This is true whether the epistle is thinking here of a profession of faith recited at baptism, or in the course of the liturgical service, which is more likely. The author is referring to the common expression of our hope, the hope namely that, by Jesus' flesh and blood, we will reach the promised goal in heaven, the " eternal inheritance " (9:15). The conviction of God's absolute fidelity and trustworthiness must banish every doubt and hesitation from our hearts.

In the early days of the church, one of the most important means of maintaining the spiritual health of the community, or of restoring it, was fraternal correction (cf. 3:13). This mutual incitement to " charity and good works " could be described as an early form of what we later came to know as the sacrament of penance, principally because it contained an element of the " comfort " which comes from the Holy Spirit. St. Paul in his letters recommends his Christians to " comfort," " encourage," and " correct " one another. This corresponds to some extent with what we today describe as the priest's " exhortation " and " absolution " in confession. As the context shows, the duty of fraternal correction and exhortation was performed especially in the liturgical assembly. Here, in the liturgical anticipation of the parousia, Christ's "day," the old idea that he is coming soon retains its lasting value as a motive. In the rest of the epistle, it has no great role to play.

A Terrible Judgment Threatens Those who Fall Away (10: 26-31)

²⁶*For if we sin deliberately, after we have received the knowledge of the truth, we have no sacrifice left for sin any more.* ²⁷*There is only the fearful expectation of the judgment and the fire which will consume those who are obstinate.* ²⁸*When anyone violated the law of Moses, he had to die without mercy on* [*the testimony*] *of two or three witnesses.* ²⁹*Surely you must realize that a man earns a worse punishment if he tramples the Son of God with his feet, profanes the blood of the covenant whereby he was made holy, and insults the Spirit of grace.* ³⁰*We know who it is that has said: " Vengeance is mine, I will repay " and again: " The Lord will judge his people "* (Deut. 32:35-36). ³¹*It is a frightful thing to fall into the hands of the living God.*

A modern Christian who reads these words, and applies them to himself, would be forced either to doubt the inerrancy of scripture or the power of God's grace. How many of us are there who do not have to confess that we have sinned deliberately after baptism and so lost sanctifying grace? But even if we " trampled the Son of God with our feet " and " insulted the Spirit of grace," the way to God's heart always remained open for us in the sacrament of penance. Does this mean that the church has abandoned the rigorous attitude of the Epistle to the Hebrews and introduced a more lenient practice? If that is so, how can our epistle really be God's word which is valid for all time? It seems to exclude the possibility of a second chance to repent. Or, to mention another possibility, has the church abandoned its original ideal of eschatological holiness? Has it reduced the grace of forgiveness which is given once and for all to the level of a " commodity " which a man can dispose of and acquire again as often as he likes? We must try to find a solution to this problem which will do justice both to the historical development of the sacrament of penance and to the theology of the Epistle to the Hebrews.

First of all, we must remember that the author of the epistle writes as a pastor who is intent on warning his flock against the danger of an apostasy which could not be made good later. He is not concerned with the problem which caused the church such trouble in later years. This was the question whether Christians who had abjured the faith in time of persecution and afterwards wanted to rejoin the church, when the danger was over, could be restored to grace once more. The fate of Christians who were guilty of capital crimes, as they were called (murder, adultery), and wanted to be received to do penance was equally difficult to decide. If our author had been confronted with this problem, he would probably have given a more carefully considered answer. In his position as it was, however, it would have been highly imprudent from a pastoral point of view to put the possibility of a second conversion before Christians who were tempted to apostasy.

To understand properly what the epistle says, we must also remember that the " deliberate " sin it warns us against so insistently must not be immediately identified with what later moral theology calls " serious " or " mortal " sin. As the example from the Old Testament shows clearly, the author is thinking primarily of apostasy from the faith and idolatry. In the sense intended by our epistle, therefore, we could say that a Christian does not sin " deliberately," or commit a crime which is unforgivable, as long as he maintains some link with Christ and the church. In our sins of " weakness " and " ignorance " (cf. 4:15), on the other hand, we can always rely on the compassionate help of our heavenly high priest. In this interpretation, the teaching of the epistle does not appear as rigorous as we often think it is, when compared with the present penitential practice of the church. On the contrary, if we take the once-and-for-all character of Christ's sin offering and its never-failing power of sanctification seriously, there can be no room for anxiety of conscience or fear regarding confession. Even the most serious " mortal sins " from a moral point of view need not imply " falling away from the living God " (3:12); we must simply let ourselves fall into his merciful hands. Then even the most terrifying moral failure can be transformed into a " profession of hope " (10:23), a hope which has no need to fear God's judgment.

CONSTANCY IN TRIALS AND PERSECUTION
(10:32—13:25)

The third part of the epistle does not seem to be as unified as the first two. As its general theme, we can perhaps best choose the exhortation: " You need endurance so that, having done God's will, you may attain the promise " (10:36; cf. 13:21). This was the way the just of the Old Testament and Jesus himself gave proof of their faith in God and his invisible city, our heavenly country. As a result, they have now attained the promised goal, at least in the person of Jesus, the "author and completer of our faith" (11:1—12:3). Temptations, struggles, suffering, and persecutions are no reason to become listless; they are part of God's plan for our training (12:4–11). The author once more contrasts the revelation of the Old Testament with that of the New Testament, to rouse his readers to a greater sense of responsibility in their moral efforts, and to religious gratitude for the eternal blessings of salvation (12:12–29). The last chapter contains a series of individual exhortations, and an " exhortatory address " (13:22). The work ends with a form of conclusion which resembles that of a letter.

A Call to Fight for the Faith (10:32—12:1)

Remember the Distress of Earlier Days (10: 32–39)

³²*Remember those earlier times when you had [just] become light and you endured a great struggle in suffering. ³³On the one hand, you were made a show of by insults and afflictions; on the other, you shared the lot of those who lived like that. ³⁴You even*

suffered with those who were prisoners and accepted the theft of your property joyfully, knowing that you yourselves had a better, a lasting possession. ³⁵Do not now throw away your authorization which brings a great reward! ³⁶You need endurance so that, having done God's will, you may attain the promise. ³⁷For " it is only a while, a very, very, short while, and he who is to come will come. He will not delay. ³⁸But my just man will live by faith. If he shrinks back, my soul takes no more pleasure in him " (Hab. 2:3f.). ³⁹We are not [the kind of men who] shrink back and are lost; we are men of faith who will earn life for ourselves.

It seems as if the author himself was suddenly frightened by the blunt threats he had made, and so he immediately changes his tone and once more addresses his listeners appealingly. As a pastor, he does not want to pass sentence on them or condemn them; he is determined to help them and bring them healing. Even though his Christians are tempted and in danger, he is able to show them a way out of their difficulties. As a good director, he advises them to recall their early days as Christians. There had been a time in their lives when they were ready to make any sacrifice for the faith. Then they were new converts, and they had endured earthly losses " with joy," because the promised goal was constantly before their eyes. But in the meantime their first fervor had evaporated; the memory of their heavenly calling which inspired them had faded away. They were lacking in the virtue of *hypomene*, endurance, patience, or perseverance, which was so highly prized at the end of the apostolic age. Instead of bravely enduring the disadvantages the Christian faith inevitably involves in this world, the readers of the epistle would have liked to throw away their *parrhesia*. They were faint-hearted and they would have preferred to renounce the right which entitled them to appear before God at any time. Did they not realize that running away was absolutely certain to bring them to ruin, although they thought it would enable them to escape? Suffering and death, on the other hand, if endured in a spirit of faith, would win them life as the prize of victory.

This is one of the few passages in the letter which contain a concrete reference to the situation in the church to which it is addressed. The expression " made a show of " (10:33) has led various commentators to suggest that the author is referring to the persecution of Nero. However, no definite conclusion can be drawn from these words and so a commentary which is intended for " spiritual reading " will do well to limit itself to the general idea. In each local church and, we hope, in the life of each Christian there must have been a period of " first love " (cf. Rev. 2:4) which it is good to look back to.

A Digression: Models of Faith (11:1—12:3)

a) A DEFINITION OF FAITH (11:1-2)

¹Faith means standing fast by the blessings we hope for, being convinced of realities which are invisible. ²It was through faith that the men of old earned a good testimony.

It is certain that the author intended giving us a definition of faith after the manner of the philosophers of the day. Yet these verses do not contain an exhaustive description of what the New Testament means by faith. The definition which is given here concerns only the idea of faith peculiar to the Epistle to the

Hebrews which is certainly very different from that of St. Paul or the synoptic gospels. For St. Paul and the gospels, faith is inextricably bound up with Jesus' person and his ministry. For our epistle, on the other hand, it is an attitude adopted towards the heavenly and invisible world which is to come. The man who is firmly convinced of the existence of this " better country " (11:13.16), this " heavenly city " (11:10.16), and refuses to be led astray by the deceptive reality of the world, gives proof of his faith. The idea of faith which we meet here is expressed in terms of a certain view of the world; it presupposes a definite theory concerning the virtues. Aiming one's life in this way at the invisible world of the heavenly blessings, for which we hope, is in keeping with the Platonist concept of being that is found in the religious philosophy of Alexandria.

This philosophical view of the world becomes faith in the Christian sense only by the addition of a profession of faith in Jesus as the " author and completer of faith " (12:2). In other words, the *pistis* (faith) defined in Hebrews chapter 11 has no immediate reference to the only form of faith which is important, namely the faith which believes that salvation has come to us in Christ. It is a virtue which could be practiced by anyone, even by good pagans such as Henoch and Noah (11:5-7), and to an exemplary degree. It does not depend on the question whether or not this longing and striving for an invisible heavenly world will be fulfilled, or by whom. Of course, the author of our epistle takes it for granted that it is Jesus who has opened the world of eternal realities to us, as God's Son and our high priest. In this way, his philosophical and religious conviction is transformed into faith in the saving significance of the cross.

A clear distinction between what faith in Jesus " really "

involves and any attempt at explaining it which is more or less dated is very important for our grasp of what it means to be a Christian today. We have confused Christian faith with a Platonist view of the world for too long, while well-founded doubts concerning the validity of this philosophical conception were regarded as a threat to the gospel. Metaphorically speaking, we have been fighting about a form of clothing which can be changed, without asking about the real nature of the object which was clothed in it. It is true that every attempt to penetrate the essence of the Christian faith is bound to date. The most we can do is to replace the old form of clothing which has become threadbare with modern dress. However, a lot would have been achieved if we Christians could even realize how relative and open to further questioning are all our theological formulas and definitions. Then we would be able to preach more convincingly about Christ who " remains the same, yesterday, today, and for ever " (13:8) to a world which is changing every day.

b) THE CREATION OF THE AEONS (11:3)

³By faith we know that the aeons were created by God's word, with the result that what is visible came from what does not appear.

The list of examples from the Old Testament begins with a verse concerning the story of creation. This gives the author another chance to clarify his philosophical concept of faith. Faith helps us to " know "; it gives us information concerning the cosmos, the real substantial relationships which exist in the world. We could turn the sentence around and say that without faith we would have no knowledge of anything except what can be seen. We would regard this as the only true reality. By faith, however, the eyes of our spirit (*nous*) are opened, so that we can almost " see " (11 : 13.27) what is invisible, God and the heavenly blessings he has promised. A Christian must have a firm hope in what is unseen; the invisible world is the direct product of God's word, while the world of experience owes its existence only to the heavenly prototypes, the " realities which do not appear." We do not know how exactly the author pictured the origin of the material world to himself. In any case, even for him the important thing was not the Alexandrine view of the universe as such; it was the need to direct our faith towards the invisible saving blessings which are to come. These have been prepared for us in heaven since the beginning of the world.

The distinction between visible realities, which must be treated with detachment if not with disdain, and the true invisible realities to which a Christian must devote himself, can still have a representative meaning today. It would be a fatal mistake, however, simply to reject visible reality as something irrelevant or even sinful, and identify the invisible ideal world with the Christian economy of salvation. The invisible God took flesh in Jesus Christ and appeared visibly on earth; since then the relation between the visible and the invisible world can never be the same. A Christian must now reckon with the fact that the invisible God himself is encountered in visible things and especially in his fellow men (cf. Mt. 25 : 31–46). It is well to bear this in mind. The emphasis in the Epistle to the Hebrews is different, but it must not be misinterpreted and understood as an invitation to despise the world because of a dualistic outlook.

c) ABEL THE JUST (11:4)

⁴It was by his faith that Abel offered a sacrifice before God which had greater value than that of Cain; by it [faith] he received a testimony that he was just. God himself bore witness concerning the gifts he offered, and by faith he [Abel] still speaks even though he is dead.

The first witness of the faith from the Old Testament is Abel. In this passage, his story is explained in the light of Christ so that he appears as a model in three respects: (1) Abel offered a sacrifice which had greater value than that of Cain, just as Christ too was able to offer a better gift than the high priests of the old covenant. The Old Testament does not say why Abel's sacrifice was better or worth more than that of Cain. The Epistle to the Hebrews takes it for granted that it was his faith which made his gift so pleasing to God. (2) Because of his sacrifice or of his faith—the text does not make it clear which— God gave his divine testimony that Abel was a just man. Faith, therefore, involves having a good testimony from God. This does away with the misconception that faith is a human achievement. The Greek verb *martyreisthai,* which we have already met as a key-word in 11:2 (cf. 11:39), makes us think of " martyrdom."

In the Epistle to the Hebrews, however, the verb does not have this technical sense, although Abel and many others who are mentioned in chapter 11 could in fact have been called " martyrs." It is obvious that the idea of a witness to the faith is not completely identical with that of a witness who sheds his blood. In the case of martyrdom, the emphasis is on what a man achieves; a martyr bears witness to God with his blood. It is the other way round with a witness to the faith. Here God bears testimony in favor of a man. With his own blood, God guarantees that the sinner has become just, that a man who was dead has risen to life. In the light of what Christ has done, we cannot express it otherwise. Faith means accepting this testimony given by God. (3) From the biblical metaphor that Abel's blood " cries out to heaven " (cf. Gen. 4:10), the author concludes—although in a very discreet formula—that Abel is still alive after death. It is a constantly recurring theme of chapter 11 that faith must prove itself in the face of death. Faith is regarded as the great power which overcomes death. Despite this, however, we cannot say that the Epistle to the Hebrews regards faith exclusively as the hope of a world to come. Christian faith surpasses all merely human presentiment of some kind of life after death, just as Jesus' blood " speaks better than Abel's blood " (12:24).

d) How Enoch Was taken Away (11:5-6)

⁵*It was by faith that Enoch was taken away, so that he never saw death; " he could not be found because God had taken him away "* (Gen. 5:24). *Before he was taken away, he received the testimony of having found favor with God.* ⁶*Without faith [it is] impossible to please [God]. The person who approaches God must believe that he is and that he will have a reward for those who seek him.*

Collections of examples for doctrinal and exhortatory purposes were very popular with public speakers in antiquity. Ecclesiasticus 44:16 quotes the example of Enoch: "Enoch lived in God's sight, and he was taken away as a model of penance for his contemporaries." In 49:14 we read: "No one else has ever arisen on earth like Enoch, and that is why he was taken away from the earth." The interest felt in the figure of Enoch, who was the subject of many popular stories, is indicated particularly by the apocalyptic books which were published under his name. He was regarded as the scribe of heaven (Jub. 4:16–21; 1 Hen. 12:3), as the one who revealed God's eschatological secrets (Jub. 4:22–24; 1 Hen. 1:3–9), and even as the mediator and guarantee of our salvation (1 Hen. 37–71). In the Epistle to the Hebrews, he is held up as the model of a faith which was revealed when he was "taken up" to God. As in the example of Abel, the emphasis is once more on victory over death. It is clear that the readers of the epistle were in danger of abandoning their faith through fear of death (cf. 2:15). They did not regard being "taken away" from the earth as something to be desired. The story of Enoch should teach them better. He was "taken away" and "carried off"; "he was found no more" among the living. Yet he had faith in God and the eternal reward he gives, and so he received an assurance that he was pleasing to God even while he was still alive. Could God allow a man in whom he was well pleased to remain dead for ever?

It is noteworthy that the expression "to approach" (cf. 4:16; 7:25; 10:1.22; 12:18) occurs once more in this context. The man who approaches God must have the faith for which Enoch was praised, if he "does not want to see death." This promise also occurs in a number of mysterious passages in the gospels (Mk. 9:1 and parall.; Jn. 8:51–52). The word "approach" comes from the liturgy. Originally it meant a person who drew near the altar in a spirit of prayer and sacrifice. It is probable that in this case we are meant to think particularly of the man who is on the point of death, who is therefore preparing to make the sacrifice of his life. It is then that we will really have need of the faith that there is a God who wants to give us a reward.

e) NOAH AND THE ARK (11:7)

⁷It was by faith that Noah was instructed about events which were not yet visible. In the fear of God, he built an ark to save his family. It was by it [faith] he condemned the world and became an heir to the justice [promised] to faith.

In the early church, Noah and the flood were favorite images of the saving power of baptism (cf. 1 Pet. 3:20). However, the Epistle to the Hebrews is not thinking back to baptism, the first step of a Christian's road to salvation; on the contrary, it looks to the future where Christians will receive that completion which is as yet invisible. Noah's faith, therefore, does not belong in the context of the process of justification which was so important for St. Paul. It is an element in the behavior of a Christian who places all his hope in God's promise of salvation, when he is confronted with the threat which death and destruction pose to his existence. Like Noah, we too have been instructed about the " realities which are not yet visible " (cf. 11:1) and, like him, we must be prepared to obey God's instructions even though we cannot see the point of them at first sight. In a commentary which is intended for spiritual reading, perhaps we would be entitled to say that, in the course of his life, a Christian builds an

" ark " for himself and his household, to save them from the avenging judgment which is to come.

However, the more immediate implication of the text is that, like Noah's behavior, the Christian faith involves a sentence of condemnation on the world with its indifference, its thoughtlessness, and its determination to live only for the day. " The Son of Man's return will be like the days of Noah. In the days before the flood, they feasted and drank, they married and were given in marriage, until the day when Noah went into the ark. They noticed nothing until the flood came and swept everything away. The return of the Son of Man will be like that " (Mt. 24 : 37–39). The condemnation of the world by faith has nothing to do with spiritual pride; the mere fact that a Christian belongs to the community of salvation does not mean that he stands head and shoulders above the " unregenerate multitude " of the non-baptized. The world on which faith passes judgment is in each one of us; it does not stop short of penetrating churches, religious houses, or ecclesiastical curias. Only the person who submits to God's judgment can hope to inherit the justification which has been promised to faith.

f) Abraham's Pilgrimage in Faith (11:8–10)

[8]*It was by faith that Abraham was called, and he obeyed the call to set out for a place which he was to receive as an inheritance, and he set out not knowing where he was going. [9]In faith, he became a squatter in the land promised to him as if it were not his own. He lived in a tent with Isaac and Jacob, heirs with him of the same promise. [10]He waited for the city which had firm foundations, of which God was the architect and the builder.*

Abraham's story contains a wealth of material to illustrate the meaning and purpose of faith. Even the way he left his native land here on earth, and his long, difficult wanderings towards an unknown goal, show us Christians that we must follow God's call blindly. Even in the promised land, which for Christians is the church, the eschatological community of salvation, we are still only squatters; we cannot settle permanently. A tent which can be folded up at any time is the symbol of a life of wandering which knows no earthly goal.

The concept of faith which is to be found in the Epistle to the Hebrews is timely and very relevant in this point. The church of the Second Vatican Council is busy abandoning its Constantinian claim to be a " house full of glory " which has been established for all time. It is preparing to assume once again the more modest role of God's tent among men, a tent which is always ready to be pitched anew in a different place, wherever God's grace calls. It remains to be seen whether or not we can still define the goal of our pilgrimage in faith as it is defined in this epistle. The image of God's city is a very ancient one, and it can still claim a place in circles where the language of the Bible is understood and loved. In an agricultural milieu, the great, golden city can still appear as the essence of all that is enticing and desirable. But what good is it to a big-city dweller, if we promise him that God " has prepared a city for him " (11:16)?

g) The Promise of Offspring (11:11–12)

[11]*It was by faith that Sarah, too, received the power to conceive, and after her child-bearing years at that. She believed that the One who promised her was faithful.* [12]*That is why, from one*

man who was dead, there has come offspring " as numerous as the stars of heaven and the sands on the sea shore which cannot be counted " (Gen. 15:5).

The second great event in the story of Abraham was the promise of offspring. It is noteworthy that the Epistle to the Hebrews celebrates Sarah's faith, whereas the Old Testament speaks rather of the way she doubted God's promise: " Sarah laughed to herself and thought: Now that I am old, will pleasure come to me again? My husband, too, is old " (Gen. 8:12). Towards the end of the apostolic age, moral exhortations in the form of rules of conduct for the various members of a household were very popular. This may have prompted our author to mention the wife (Sarah), rather than the husband (Abraham), when he speaks about begetting offspring (cf. 1 Tim. 2:15). However, many Christians had become doubtful and uncertain and it is possible that the author deliberately put before them the example of a woman who, as they were well aware, was finally convinced of the truth and credibility of God's word only when his promise had been fulfilled. The Christians of the first century could only know by faith that from one Man who died on the cross an innumerable multitude would receive salvation and life. This had already occurred symbolically in the case of Abraham. As far as his ability to beget children was concerned, the patriarch had already been long dead, yet by God's promise he became the father of what the Bible regards as an unimaginably great people. Death is not an insurmountable obstacle for faith; this is the constant theme of our letter. Indeed, it was only by their death that the witnesses of the faith in the old covenant attained the promised goal in heaven.

h) THE HEAVENLY COUNTRY (11:13–16)

¹³It was in faith that they all died without having attained the promises. They only saw them from afar and hailed them. They acknowledged that they were only strangers and travelers on earth. ¹⁴Those who say such things make it known that they are looking for a country of their own. ¹⁵If they had been thinking of the country from which they set out, they would have had plenty of time to go back. ¹⁶But as it was, they sought after a better, a heavenly country. That is why God is not ashamed of them, or that he should be called their God. He has prepared a city for them.

The author has not yet finished with the examples which he quotes from the story of Abraham and the patriarchs (cf. 11:17–22). However, he digresses here, to sum up the fate of those who were determined to be nothing more than strangers and travelers on earth. The patriarchs were semi-nomadic and they traveled about constantly, changing their pasturage according to the season of the year. It is clear, however, that the author is not thinking exclusively of them; he is thinking of all the faithful. This earth can never be their final home. There is no other passage of the epistle in which the author's dualistic nostalgia is so forcibly and so movingly expressed as here. These verses have become classic, and they have given a decisive stamp to our Christian view of life right down to the present day. What the author says here about our heavenly country seems to us to be an inalterable element in our Christian vocabulary; we regard it as one of the most important truths of our faith. To call it into doubt would be like abandoning the gospel. This is all the more reason why we will be surprised to hear that there is no other passage of the Bible in which heaven is described as man's true home, but that this idea occurs again and again in Philo of Alexandria. As usual, this is not one of Philo's own ideas; he merely adopts a conception which was an expression of the Greek dualism of spirit and body. In a system in which man's self (or his spirit or soul) is regarded as a preëxistent heavenly being, heaven must naturally be understood as his real home; it was only as the result of some cosmic mishap that man fell to the level of evil matter such as the flesh. Did the Epistle to the Hebrews make this dualistic concept of existence a truth of revelation, so that it must be blessed for all time? Various Christian funeral hymns which speak of man's true home as being above, in the realm of light, would certainly lead us to think so.

The fact is, however, that this is only a way of speaking which is now outdated. It is intended merely to illustrate the truth that man exists for God and for the goal God sets him. In our own day, we would certainly use other means to describe the goal of our human journey in the faith; we would not use the Alexandrine idea of a heavenly country, or the apocalyptic concept of a city of God. A modern Christian realizes that he has obligations to this earth; he does not look for a home among the stars. What we still have is the hope that God will acknowledge us as his own, as he acknowledged the patriarchs, although he has every reason to be ashamed of us.

i) The Sacrifice of Isaac (11:17–19)

17It was in faith that Abraham offered up Isaac, when he was tested; he offered up his first-born, he who had received the promises [18]*and was told: " In Isaac your descendants will be named "* (Gen. 21:12). [19]*He realized that God had power to raise from the dead. And he did receive him back symbolically.*

The moving account of the sacrifice of Isaac is reëchoed in a variety of interpretations in the New Testament. St. Paul (Rom. 8:32) and St. John (Jn. 3:16) interpret the figure of Abraham as an image of God the Father who gave up his Only-Begotten for us (cf. Gen. 22:16). In contrast to this strictly theological interpretation, the Epistle to the Hebrews concentrates on the attitude of a man of faith from whom God demands precisely what he has just given him, or promised him. In this trial, Abraham believed in God against God. The Epistle to the Hebrews regards his faith as the conclusion of a logical process of reasoning: If God has power to raise the dead, he can also demand the death of the heir to the promise. Therefore, Abraham could have gone ahead with his blood offering, and if he did receive his only son back in an unbloody manner, it was only a " symbol " of the true life which we receive once more after death.

The author of our letter was not concerned with the moral scruples of a man like Kierkegaard. Kierkegaard remarks that God demanded something of Abraham which was immoral, the murder of an innocent person. Abraham should have refused to obey this unjust command. At the present time, it is possible that the real test of a man's faith may be found in some such conflict between authority and the moral law. We cannot imagine that God would demand something immoral of a man. The facile apologetic explanation that, after all, God is the Lord of life and death, is not entirely sufficient. The truth is that the story concerns child-sacrifice, something which the God of the Old Testament abhorred and strictly forbad, in contrast to the pagan deities of the Canaanites. In this context, Abraham's willingness to obey the divine command creates a serious problem. The story is an etiological account which was intended to provide a basis for the prohibition of child-sacrifice in Israel; what God really wanted becomes clear only at the end: " Do the boy no harm " (Gen. 22:12). But what have these considerations to do with the faith which is the theme of Hebrews 11? More than we would perhaps think at first sight. They can warn us against identifying the Christian faith with the frightful delusion which kindled funeral pyres, laid waste whole countries, and massacred innocent children without pity, all in the name of God and supposedly at his command. The rallying-cry " God wills it " must always be used with the greatest caution. Otherwise we may blindly offer sacrifice to idols and demons, instead of to the one, true, and holy God.

j) THE PATRIARCHS' BLESSINGS (11:20–22)

²⁰*It was through faith in what was to come that Isaac blessed Jacob and Esau. *²¹*By faith Jacob blessed each of Joseph's sons when he was dying, and worshiped [God] as [he bowed] over the top of his staff. *²²*It was in faith that Joseph, at his death, looked forward to the departure of the sons of Israel and made arrangements for his mortal remains.*

The connecting thought in this short section is once more the conquest of the future in the face of death. The text alludes to the dying patriarch's last words; this was a favorite literary form in antiquity. The last words of a dying man were regarded as being endowed with special power. This universal human conviction found expression in eloquent speeches which gave the writer an opportunity to explain the present in the light of the past. In the book of Genesis, such last words are found especially in the form of blessings or curses pronounced by the patriarchs. A blessing pronounced by a father or mother at the point of death is naturally a precious treasure for their child; a final curse, on the other hand, would seem to involve inevitable misfortune. For the Bible, a blessing or a curse has a power which is almost sacramental; it effects what the words say. The Epistle to the Hebrews interprets this power which is capable of deciding the future in advance as faith. It must certainly appear paradoxical that, in his whole life, a man never has greater power over the future (in faith!) than he has precisely at the moment when he is threatened with the loss of it by death. What the patriarchs did on their death beds confirms the definition which the Epistle to the Hebrews (11:1) clothes in an abstract formula: " Faith means holding fast to realities which are to come, and being convinced of things which are invisible."

k) Moses' Example of Faith (11:23-28)

[23]*It was in faith that Moses was kept hidden for three months as a child by his parents, because they saw that he was a lovely child. They were not afraid of the king's command.* [24]*It was in faith that Moses refused to be called " the son of Pharaoh's daughter," when he grew up.* [25]*He chose to suffer hardship with the People of God, in preference to enjoying the passing pleasures of sin.* [26]*He regarded Christ's shame as a greater treasure than all the wealth of Egypt. He looked forward to the bestowal of the*

reward. ²⁷It was in faith that he left Egypt; he was not afraid of the king's hostility. He held fast by him who is invisible as if he could see him. ²⁸In faith he established the Passover and the sprinkling of blood, so that the angel who destroyed the first-born children would not harm those who were protected.

In the example of Moses which is developed in great detail, the idea of martyrdom comes to the forefront more clearly, the steadfastness of the witnesses of the faith in a world which persecuted them. Even Moses' parents gave proof of their steadfast faith; they fearlessly refused to comply with the king's edict and saved their child from certain death. For them, his good looks were a sign of divine predilection. Moses was educated at the Egyptian court, but he refused to pass for the adopted son of the king's daughter and share the pleasures of a life of luxury. Instead, he threw in his lot with his own persecuted and enslaved people and bore " Christ's shame " (cf. 13 : 13), as the epistle says in a conscious effort to make the Old Testament story more actual. Then he defied the king and led the people fearlessly out of Egypt.

Verse 28 mentions the institution of the Passover as the last of the deeds he performed in faith, together with the blood rite which was intended to ward off evil spirits (Ex. 12 : 7.13). In this case, it served to protect the Israelites' first-born children from the avenging angel. The verse is constructed in such an unusual way that we might almost think it was Moses' own blood which was involved in this sprinkling. Moses' conduct is obviously presented as being parallel to the story of Christ's passion. The institution of the Passover is followed by the sprinkling of the blood which brings salvation. The examples which follow this passage (11 : 29–31) mention the redemption of the chosen people.

In the story of Moses as it is recounted in this epistle, the readers could easily see the story of their own lives. They, too, were threatened with heavy penalties by royal and imperial laws; like the Israelites in Egypt, they too had to endure injustices and humiliations. Presumably the church included Christians from aristocratic circles; their good connections would have made it possible for them to preserve themselves and their dependants from all harm. Moses' example was intended to make it clear to all of these that a Christian can transgress a human ordinance without fear, if only he keeps the invisible God and his heavenly reward before his eyes (cf. 11:6). Besides the obvious exhortatory character of the passage, did the author also intend to portray Moses as Christ? Was this not perhaps even his primary intention? In that case, Moses who was hidden by his parents as a child would be a type of the child Jesus who was persecuted by Herod. This is the line taken by the infancy gospel of St. Matthew. The Christological interpretation of Moses as an adult is even more obvious. He renounced the title of king's son, to share the sufferings of his people and endure "Christ's shame." In the same way, Christ divested himself of his glory as God's Son and became like us human beings in our suffering (2:5-18; cf. Philem. 2:5-11). Finally, what was only hinted at in Moses' celebration of the paschal meal, and the mysterious blood rite, was fulfilled for all time in Christ's atoning death—the definitive redemption of the People of God from the onslaught of sin and death.

l) EXAMPLES OF MIRACULOUS ESCAPES AND EARTHLY SUCCESS (11:29-35a)

[29]*It was in faith that they passed through the Red Sea as over*

dry land, while the Egyptians, when they made the same
attempt, were swamped. ³⁰*In faith, the walls of Jericho came*
tumbling down after they had spent seven days walking around
them. ³¹*It was in faith that Rahab the prostitute escaped destruc-*
tion with those who did not obey; she welcomed the scouts in
peace. ³²*What more can I say? Time would fail me, if I were*
to speak of Gideon, Barak, Samson, Jephthah, David, Samuel,
and the prophets. ³³*They brought down kingdoms by faith, and*
put justice to work. They obtained the promises, and stopped
the jaws of lions. ³⁴*They quenched the power of fire, and escaped*
the sword's mouth. In their weakness, they were filled with
strength. They became heroes in war, and forced the ranks of
foreign [armies] to break. ³⁵ᵃ*Women received their dead back*
when they were raised to life.

Despite their lack of formal unity, we have grouped these verses
together in one passage because they illustrate a theme which
is clearly at variance with the idea of faith in this chapter. Up
to this—and once more at the end of the chapter—the witnesses
of the faith were pilgrims, strangers, and outcasts; they were
persecuted and martyred in this world. They had to die to bear
witness to the fact that a man whom God has called finds his
true home in heaven. Now, however, the picture is different.
The suffering and pilgrim People of God have become the
ecclesia triumphans, the church which triumphs over its enemies
by God's miraculous power. The Israelites pass dry-shod through
the sea; the Egyptians are drowned. The walls of Jericho
collapse and only a prostitute who had shown the spies hospitality is saved; all the other inhabitants of the city are killed.
In the case of these first three examples, we may ask whether
the same idea of faith is still maintained, holding fast by what

is invisible and hoping for something which is to come. In the miracles which accompanied the exodus and the occupation of Canaan, the Israelites had practical experience of a salvation which was present in palpable form. They were the successful ones; their " faith " helped them to overcome earthly difficulties in a miraculous manner.

The contrast between the idea of faith which has been presented in previous chapters and the summary account of the " success stories " of the Old Testament is even more noticeable. Various heroic deeds, military victories, and miraculous escapes from death are mentioned together with achievements of a political or social nature and the raising of the dead to life, without any exact chronological or objective order. It is easy to understand that public orators in antiquity liked to celebrate what was unusual, spectacular, or surprising. Even the gospel illustrates the greatness of faith by its power to " move mountains " (Mk. 11:23; Mt. 17:20); we can hardly blame the Epistle to the Hebrews because of its drastic examples. However, we must ask what becomes of the invisible character of the redemption which is to come, if it is true that the witnesses of the faith " attained the promises," and " escaped the sword's mouth "? We have no idea why the author chose these examples which are not really in keeping with his idea of faith. He probably wanted to encourage his persecuted readers in their trials, by reminding them that God occasionally comes to the aid of his faithful in a miraculous manner. It may be, however, that he merely incorporated an already existing list of examples into his text without noticing that for the faithful any visible fulfillment of God's promise can never be anything more than a symbol and a sign of a higher, invisible reality.

These verses are particularly important for the problem of

faith today. We Christians have learned that faith is not a miraculous or a magic means to make life easier or do away with the uncomfortable realities of the world. The walls of Jericho will not be brought down today by a procession or a blast of trumpets. On the other hand, this realization has not led to an attitude of resigned indifference to the world and its tasks; on the contrary, it has strengthened the conviction that faith must prove itself in our visible circumstances here and now. The only thing is that the signs which faith will show to the world today will differ from those it showed in the days of Gideon, Barak, Samson, or Samuel.

m) THE MARTYRS OF THE OLD COVENANT (11:35b-38)

35bOthers were tortured, because they refused to accept a pardon, so that they might share in a better resurrection. 36Others again were familiar with insults and scourgings, and even chains and imprisonment. 37They were stoned, burned, and cut in pieces; they were put to death by the sword. They went about in sheepskins or goatskins, enduring bitter distress. They were afflicted and ill-treated. 38The world was not worthy of them, and they wandered about in deserts and among the mountains, in caves and ravines on the earth.

It is as if the author suddenly remembered the distinctions he had made; he abandons his "success stories" and turns once more to the sufferings endured by the witnesses of the faith. Earthly consolations may be good, but faith knows a "better" hope. It is this which makes it worthwhile enduring all the pain and distress of this world (cf. Rom. 8:18). It is impossible to say what persons or events of the Old Testament or the apocryphal literature the author had in mind in writing his " martyrology." For one thing, the text of verse 37 is uncertain. The prophet Zechariah, who was a son of the priest Jehoiada, was " stoned," for example (2 Chron. 24:20–22; cf. Mt. 23:35–37); Isaiah was " cut in pieces," according to one legendary tradition (*Ascension of Isaiah*, 5:11–14). The death of a number of prophets by the sword is mentioned in 1 Kings 19:10. The important thing, however, is not the identity of the individual persons; it is the realization that this list of sufferings is intended to be characteristic of the Christian life.

A Christian is conscious that he is different. Consequently, he may be tempted either to shun the conflict with the world, or to raise it to the level of a principle. A particularly seductive form of shunning this conflict would be to withdraw voluntarily into a pious ghetto, into the peaceful exile of self-chosen renunciation. Going about in " sheepskins " or " goatskins " and sneaking off into " deserts " or " ravines " can become a vogue; it need not necessarily be a sign of faith. Equally sterile is the attitude which raises opposition to the world to the level of a principle. The Epistle to the Hebrews obviously takes it for granted that the martyrs encountered the fatal opposition of the world because of their faith. But what exactly is " faith "? Surely this is a question which must always be examined anew and given a fresh answer. It would be only too easy to hold up basic rejection of the world, a sort of nonconformism in principle, as a form of faith. Only too often in the course of history have wrong attacks been launched against the wrong lines. Stubbornness, obstinacy, and intellectual laziness have often been mistaken for an unshakable faith. The " world " which persecutes and torments us, insulting us and holding us in bonds, does not always have to be on the side of the "others," the unbelievers and the godless; we must look for it in ourselves first of all.

n) CONCLUDING REMARKS CONCERNING THE MARTYRS (11:39–40)

39Yet, all these did not attain the promise, [although] faith bore them witness. 40With us in mind, God had provided something better, so that they would not be completed without us.

The just of the old law had the exact same goal before their eyes as we Christians have. The same promise had been made to them as to us, the promise of a heavenly city of God, an ever-lasting country. This "world to come" (2:5) had been prepared since the beginning of creation, but no one could enter it. Jesus, the heavenly high priest and God's Son, opened a way there for the human race, as their precursor and pontifex. It was through him that the just of the Old Testament, too, were to be completed, that is, to attain their heavenly goal.

We have no right to expect exact information from our letter concerning the individual stages or the time of this eschatological fulfillment. Faith in the immortality of the soul and the hope of the resurrection, together with the particular and the general judgment, had as yet scarcely been seen in their particular perspectives and no attempt had been made to reconcile them. So it is not clear, for example, what exactly happened the just of the Old Testament after their death, or when the "spirits of the just who were completed" (12:23) entered the heavenly Jerusalem. Equally difficult to answer is the question how exactly the author pictured to himself the "completion" enjoyed

by Christians who had died. Did he believe that they entered
the heavenly sanctuary immediately after death, following in the
footsteps of their heavenly high priest, or that they had to wait
for the parousia? Very likely he made no effort whatever to
consider things systematically; he simply put the various themes
which were known to him from Jewish, Christian, or Hellenistic
tradition side by side, according as they fitted into the context.
This unsystematic approach is probably more in keeping with
the subject of such eschatological discourses than any far-fetched
attempt to draw up an exact " timetable " for the events which
will mark the end of time; it leaves in the dark what—as far as
we are concerned—happens in the dark.

o) THE AUTHOR AND COMPLETER OF FAITH (12:1–3)

*¹So, then, as we have such a cloud of witnesses surrounding us,
we are determined to cast off all that encumbers us and the sin
which clings to us so easily. We must run with endurance in the
contest which lies before us, ²with our gaze fixed on Jesus, the
author and completer of faith. For the sake of the joy which lay
before him, he bore the cross and paid no attention to the shame,
and has taken his place at the right of God's throne. ³Think of
him! He bore such opposition from sinners. Then you will not
be weary and despairing in your souls.*

The list of the witnesses of the faith in the Old Testament, and
the various sufferings they endured, is at an end. The epistle
once more addresses the persecuted community, to encourage
them to persevere in their hard struggle for the faith. The metaphor of a race is familiar to us from St. Paul and also from

secular literature. Ordinary people were enthusiastic about sport even in antiquity. We are probably meant to picture the cloud of witnesses as spectators who follow the exciting contest from the sideline. Ordinary common sense will prompt a runner to throw off everything which could hold him back or trip him up. From an ascetic point of view, this is a suggestive thought, presupposing, of course, that the will to fight is there. It seems that it was precisely in this that the local church to which the Epistle to the Hebrews is addressed was lacking; they had forgotten that the prize of victory could only be won after a hard struggle.

Here once more we meet the key word "endurance" (*hypomone*; cf. 10:36). The greatest example of such enduring, suffering, and patient faith is Jesus who was crucified and raised up to God. Christians who have become tired and weary must fix their eyes unwaveringly on him. It was only in him that the whole series of martyrs and witnesses of the faith from the Old Testament attained their goal. He is the " completer of faith," because by his death he brought the promises made to such faith to fulfillment; he made them a visible reality. Without Jesus, all human wandering, running, and struggling are in vain; they would never reach their goal. Only Jesus can complete the faith, because he alone is its " author," its " beginner," and its " source."

The word *archaegos* (" author," " prince ") is not easy to translate into English. It refers not merely to Jesus' " princely " function as a leader who precedes his brothers, all the redeemed, into their heavenly inheritance, but also to his preëxistence in the world of the heavenly archetypes as the Son and the mediator of creation. In philosophical terms, we can say that Jesus is the basis for the possibility of faith as it is understood in the Epistle to the Hebrews; he is our surety that such faith will not be vain. By his own example, Jesus has shown us how the shame and disgrace of the cross and a violent death lead to eternal happiness and glory. Ordinary common sense should make Christians who are in danger of becoming tired of the struggle realize that it would be utter stupidity to give up. How could they hope to win eternal happiness without " having to endure the opposition of sinners "?

God's Wisdom in Training Us (12:4-11)

⁴*You have not yet resisted to the point of bloodshed, as you struggle against sin.* ⁵*You have forgotten the exhortation which addresses you as sons: " My son, do not scorn the Lord's discipline or become faint, when you are punished by him.* ⁶*For it is the person whom the Lord loves that he disciplines. He scourges every son whom he welcomes"* (Prov. 3:11-12). ⁷*Endure this " discipline "; God is treating you as " sons." Where is there a " son" whose father does not discipline him?* ⁸*If you are left without any of the discipline which everyone has to share, you must be bastards, not sons.* ⁹*Moreover, we had our earthly fathers to discipline us, and we revered them. Shall we not be much more submissive to the Father of spirits and life?* ¹⁰*They punished us only for a short time at their own whim, while he [punishes us] for our good, so that we may share his holiness.* ¹¹*Certainly, for the moment, all discipline seems to cause sorrow, not joy, but it later brings those accustomed to it holiness and peace.*

It is becoming more and more clear that the local church addressed in the Epistle to the Hebrews shrank back in terror at the thought of persecutions and suffering. They had formed a less complicated idea of what it meant to be a Christian; they thought that a child of God had a claim on the protection of his heavenly Father. Even the gospel story of Jesus' temptations in the desert (Mt. 4:1-11; Lk. 4:1-13) is directed against this pagan conception of the relationship between God the Father and his child. It is easy to see that any good pagan would expect his Father in heaven, before all else, to preserve him from distress in this world and rescue him miraculously from any threat to his life. But the fate which his " author and completer " endured should be enough to make a Christian think otherwise. God's Son had to " learn obedience by what he suffered " (5:8), and God trains his other sons in the hard school of suffering, in the same way. The context suggests and even demands this Christological comparison; yet the author contents himself with a rationalistic-sounding quotation from the Book of Proverbs; God behaves like any sensible father who wants to make something of his children. Trials and suffering, therefore, are not a sign of God's anger; they are a proof of his fatherly love and care.

This point of view is stressed in numerous passages of the Old Testament but unfortunately it is not deeply rooted in the minds of Christians today. An exaggerated and one-sided emphasis on the doctrine of original sin has led us, without more ado, to ascribe all the sufferings and difficulties of life to the fall of our first parents. Such an explanation is unworthy; it makes God out to be a fairy-tale figure, and deprives human suffering of its dignity as a task for which we must take personal responsibility. This is precisely the end at which the Epistle to the Hebrews aims with its solution to the problem of suffering. In the trials which he sends them, the author wants his readers to feel that God is treating them as his " sons." They must be made

to realize that the hard discipline the " Father of the spirits "
sends them is for their good. Of course, there are also other
points of view in the New Testament which at first sight might
seem " more theological." We read of the " sufferings which
are characteristic of the last stage of time," of " sharing Christ's
sufferings," and even of the consequences of personal sins (for
example, 1 Cor. 11 : 30). However, the idea developed in our
epistle has the advantage of being immediately clear to everybody, and it is something which can be accomplished without
any form of religious exaggeration.

Sharing Pastoral Responsibility (12:12–17)

¹²*Therefore, you must straighten your failing hands and your
shaking knees once more.* ¹³*Make a straight path for your feet,
so that what is lame already may not be dislocated, but be made
sound.* ¹⁴*Keep peace with all men, and the holiness without
which no one will see the Lord.* ¹⁵*Keep watch, so that no one
may fall short of God's grace, or some bitter root grow up and
cause unrest, so that the many are defiled.* ¹⁶*No one is to be
lascivious or profane like Esau who sold his birthright for a
single meal.* ¹⁷*You know how he was afterwards rejected when
he wanted to inherit the blessing; he was given no place for
repentance, even though he asked for it with tears.*

The final exhortation and warning which the epistle addresses
to the whole local community emphasizes the common pastoral
responsibility of all the faithful. It is not only that each individual must strive after peace and holiness; the community as such
has an obligation to " keep watch," for the spiritual health of
all its members. The duty of " overseeing " which was later

concentrated in the office of the *episcopos* (" overseer ") or bishop is here regarded as something involving the whole church. Like every disciplinary measure in the church, the duty to " keep watch " is intended to promote the well-being and the sanctification of the members who are sick, and preserve those who are in health from being infected.

Three wrongful courses of conduct are mentioned. In the present critical situation of the community they were particularly dangerous, and could easily lead to final reprobation: (1) ". . . that no one may fall short of God's grace." The author has already warned his readers in a previous passage (4:1) against the danger of " falling short," " coming too late," or " being excluded." There it was entry into God's heavenly rest, the eternal goal promised us, that was at stake. In the present passage, the faithful are warned to be careful that no one falls short " behind God's grace." This formula has a very general sound, but it is far from clear. If the warning was addressed to individual Christians, it could perhaps be interpreted in the sense of modern ascetical theology: A Christian must not fail to respond to the inspirations of grace; he must not exclude himself from the state of grace by mortal sin. However, this passage of the epistle deals with the obligation of keeping watch which binds the whole community. Therefore, " God's grace " must be understood as an objective, concrete reality. Could we say that God's grace is to be found where the " throne of grace " (4:16) is set up, and the " spirit of grace " (10:29) makes its presence felt, that is, in the common liturgical worship? Then the exhortation would mean simply: Take care that no one excludes himself from the place of grace which has now been made accessible (cf. 10:25), so that he will not be forced to remain behind when God distributes the " blessing," his eternal saving grace, at the judgment. (2) ". . . that no bitter root may grow up and cause unrest, so that the many are defiled." This metaphor goes back to Deuteronomy 29:18 where idolaters are compared to a root which grows up to produce poison and gall. Instead of " in gall " (*en cholae*), our epistle has: " to cause unrest " (*encholae*). What is meant is any behavior that causes disturbance and harms the good name of the community, that can have a pernicious influence on others. There is no need to take this as referring only to apostasy from the faith and relapse into idolatry, as in Deuteronomy. Any member of the church can be a "bitter root," if he gives scandal and leads others into sin by his refusal to be satisfied, his complaining, and his unworthy maneuvering. (3) ". . . that no one is lascivious or profane like Esau who sold his birthright for a single meal." In the Old Testament, fornication and other forms of debauchery often serve as a symbol of idolatry which, at that time, involved orgiastic fertility cults and extravagant feasting. Therefore, this verse too could be interpreted as a warning against apostasy and relapse into paganism. However, apostasy from the faith is not always a straightforward affair such as voluntarily " leaving the church " in a visible way. It can also exist in the form of a terribly harmful behavior within the community. In that case, it is the duty of the " overseer " to exclude such destructive and harmful elements, if there is no sign of improvement (cf. Mt. 18:15).

If this situation is presupposed, the hard saying about Esau " not finding an opportunity to repent," although he " sought it with tears," becomes clear. The phrase a " place " or " space " for repentance (*topos metanoias*) is a technical term in the theory of repentance. It means the objective possibility of conversion which is a gift from God. Such a " space for repentance " is always limited in time. God alone appoints its beginning and

its end. Our modern psychological conception of repentance forgets this fundamental fact too easily; it makes repentance dependent on the good will of man. There is such a thing, therefore,
as being " too late "; the opportunity may be missed, so that it
can never be recovered, even with tears of repentance. There can
be no doubt about the moment of time our epistle has in mind.
It is the moment of Judgment, when God (or, in the present
context, Isaac) distributes his blessing or pronounces a sentence
of condemnation. Then an Esau Christian will plead with tears
and cries of sorrow for a further " space for repentance "; but
God can no longer give him any such chance. The revelation
which came in Christ is God's last and final offer of grace for
the human race and the whole of creation.

Judgment and Grace (12:18–29)

This section can be described without exaggeration as the
rhetorical climax of the epistle. Even the construction is artistic
in the extreme: it mirrors on a smaller scale the technique
followed in the whole composition. The theological presentation
of the author's doctrine (vv. 18–24) is followed by an exhortation
which draws the practical conclusions from it (vv. 25–29). Both
these sections are further subdivided: The theological text contrasts the divine revelation contained in the Old Testament with
that of the New Testament; the exhortation starts with a warning and a threat and ends with an encouraging promise. Therefore, even the articulation of the passage shows to what extent
the author thinks in contrasts. He puts together the present time
and the time to come, earth and heaven, what is transient and
what is unchanging, to form one powerful image, and make
his Christians realize the gravity of their situation.

¹⁸*For it is not a visible [mountain] that you have approached, with a blazing fire accompanied by smoke and darkness and storm.* ¹⁹*There was no trumpet-blast or noise of words, at which the hearers begged that the word might not be addressed to them again.* ²⁰*They could not bear the provision that: " If even a beast touches the mountain, it must be stoned"* (Ex. 19:13). ²¹*The display of nature's forces was so frightening that Moses said: " I am afraid and trembling "* (Deut. 9:19).

To reduce the contrast between the Sinai covenant and the covenant of Sion to denominators such as fear and terror on the one hand, and grace and glory on the other, would be to over-simplify. If that was all there was to it, why should God be referred to as the " Judge of all," in the context of the saving blessings of the New Testament? Why should the exhortations contained in the New Testament threaten Christians who are disobedient with a judgment far more terrible than that which fell on the unbelieving Israelites in the desert? We saw before that this epistle is not directed against the Jews; on the contrary, it is intended to encourage its Christian readers whose faith was weak, by appealing to proofs from scripture. In the image of Isaac's blessing (12:17), we have already seen the Last Judgment, in which God will decide irrevocably who is to inherit salvation. This passage, too, deals with the revelation of God's judgment. Despite the visible and terrifying phenomena which accompanied the revelation of God's judgment on Mount Sinai, and even because of them, we must say that it was provisional. The revelation of God's judgment in the Christian church, however, is definitive, despite its invisible and heavenly attractive character, and even because of it. Consequently, the risk is all the greater, if it results in a condemnation. The description of the revelation on Mount Sinai is noteworthy in many respects. It is true that the different details are taken from the Old Testament, but the way the author chooses them and puts them together betrays his fixed intention to reduce the Sinaitic revelation to a visible natural phenomenon. There is no mention whatever of God himself; he is completely hidden behind the visible phenomena which displayed and at the same time concealed his terrifying power. In the same way, the epistle makes no mention of the exalted moral tone of the decalogue, or of the intimacy with God to which Moses was invited. This shows that the author did not want to give an exhaustive description of what happened on Mount Sinai; he merely wanted to emphasize its essentially external and visible nature.

The terrifying phenomena which accompanied the revelation on Mount Sinai—fire, thunder and lightning, earthquakes, and the trumpet-blast—are stereotyped elements in Old Testament theophanies. God's coming at the Last Judgment is described in the same terms. It is particularly in the enthronement psalms, as they are called (Ps. 93; 96; 97; 99), that we find God's intervention as a judge in the present and in time to come associated with the natural phenomena which occurred on Mount Sinai. We must not be surprised, therefore, if the Epistle to the Hebrews shortens the perspective and interprets what happened on Mount Sinai as a threat of judgment which was immediately executed.

The command to stay away from the mountain (Ex. 19:12.13) was obviously quite a secondary matter when compared with the giving of the law. Yet the Epistle to the Hebrews takes it as being characteristic of the Old Testament revelation in general. Approaching God really meant "not being able to approach him," just as drawing near to God in worship really meant staying away from him and remaining outside (9: 7–8), because of the division in the sanctuary. The exaggerated and one-sided reproduction of Exodus 19: 12–13 is intended to underline drastically the fact that the Old Testament was limited to the domain of the flesh. The text of Exodus 19: 12–13 mentions only human beings and domesticated animals in the command to stay away from the mountain, but the Epistle to the Hebrews extends it even to wild animals. However, our author regarded this command as being important primarily because we are told that its violation involved immediate punishment.

22But you have approached Mount Sion and the city of the living God, the heavenly Jerusalem, with its myriads of angels, a festive gathering. 23You have approached the assembly of the firstborn whose names are written in heaven, and God the universal Judge, together with the spirits of the just who are completed, 24and the mediator of a new covenant, Jesus, as well as the blood which was sprinkled and speaks better than Abel. 25See to it that you do not reject him who is speaking! Indeed, if those did not escape who rejected him as he made himself known on earth, we certainly shall not escape, if we turn away from him as he speaks from heaven. 26His voice then made the earth tremble, but now he promised: " Just once more, and I will make not only the earth, but heaven also tremble" (Hag. 2: 6). 27The words " just once more" imply that what is shaken will disappear, because it is created, so that only what cannot be shaken will remain. 28We have been given a kingdom which cannot be shaken, and so we must give thanks. In so doing, we will serve God in a way pleasing to him, in reverent awe. 29Our God is certainly a consuming fire.

The author's peculiar approach to the Sinaitic revelation, in

which he views it in an eschatological light as a divine sentence
of punishment, is wholly subordinate to the contrasting picture
he paints of the New Testament revelation. Here, too, we see
that points of time and space which are far apart are juxtaposed,
to form a grandiose image of all that is essential in the Christian
life. For his treatment of the Old Testament, the author took
one concrete historical event. This makes it all the more surprising that he now passes over Jesus' ministry completely. He who
speaks to us from heaven (12:25) is God. If this is a reference
to Christ's mediation in revelation, which cannot be completely
excluded (cf. 1:2), it means that the revelation brought to us by
the Son has been transposed into a timelessly valid present (cf.
13:8). But the heavenly words from God which the Epistle to
the Hebrews has in mind are not an event of the past or the
historic present; they belong to the future. They are the divine
voice which will make heaven and earth tremble at the Last
Judgment, so that the visible creation which has passed away
will be replaced by a kingdom which cannot be shaken (12:27).
This revelation is still to come, and yet it is already present in
the inviolable character of the promise. Where we have God's
word, differences of time are not essential. We have a striking
example of this in the formula used in 12:26b: "But now (in
the present) he promised (past): Just once more, and I will . . ."
(future).

With the Christian church things are different. Here there is
a clear reference to something in the past: You have approached.
At our first encounter with God's eternal blessings in baptism
a lasting bond is forged which we experience anew in the
common celebration of the liturgy where we express our gratitude (12:28). There what we await at the Last Judgment is
already accomplished; we receive a kingdom which cannot be

shaken. Therefore, past, present, and future are all rolled into one even for the church as a whole. By approaching in faith, Christians have already left the judgment and the end of the world behind them. If they turn back and refuse to believe, they will call down on themselves immediately the judgment which is to come.

Salvation or condemnation is decided here and now by faith in God's eschatological promise. The church has already made its approach; consequently, the cosmic transformation has already taken place for Christians. They are beyond the visible, transient world. In the same way, those who have refused belief are already involved in the final catastrophe, because they have turned back to things which can be shaken. However, as the New Testament revelation—in contrast to the Old—is primarily a sentence of recompense which leads to the glory of an eternal kingdom (cf. Mt. 25:34), the drama must always close, both here and in eternity, on a note of adoration and gratitude (12:28). Ultimately, therefore, two forms of activity which are parallel are described in this section (cf. 10:19–21). Or, better, the same eschatological activity takes place in a twofold way, here and now as a liturgical preview of what is to come, in the future as the historical and definitive reality of eternity; here and now as a promise, then as fulfillment. If we consider the one, indivisible, heavenly reality, however, there is no difference; Christians already possess what is essential in the realities which cannot be shaken (10:1). The presence of what is to come and the sight of what is invisible have always been a vital element in religious practice, as was the poetic intuition of the unity of time, space, and action. In Christian worship, these have become a genuine reality which is welcomed in a spirit of gratitude and reverence.

An Exhortation to Live a Christian Life (13:1-6)

¹*Let brotherly love remain!* ²*Do not forget to be hospitable. In this way, many have given shelter to angels, without realizing it.* ³*Remember those who are in prison, because you share their bondage, and those who endure privation, because you too are still in your mortal flesh.* ⁴*Marriage [must be] respected by everyone, and the marriage bed must not be violated. God will judge fornicators and adulterers.* ⁵*Your lives [must be] free from avarice. Be content with what is at hand. God himself told us: "I will never abandon you; I will never forsake you"* (Deut. 31:6.8; Josh. 1:5). ⁶*This gives us the courage to say: "The Lord is my helper; I shall not be afraid. What can a man do to me?"* (Ps. 118:6).

The last chapter of the epistle seems almost like a later addition. The tone is calmer, and the sentences are smoother and more sober. However, it would be against the author's whole makeup if he failed to provide a profound theological reason for even the simplest exhortation. He says that brotherly love must "remain." This certainly does not mean simply that the faithful must be outstanding for their effective charity, as in former times (cf. 6:10; 10:33). Whenever the epistle speaks of something "remaining," it is always thinking of the heavenly blessings which "remain" for ever (7:3.24; 10:34; 12:27; 13:14). Love is the principal among the blessings which are imperishable (cf. 1 Cor. 13:13).

The appeal for hospitality also has reference to the heavenly world. The Old Testament tells us that angels sometimes appeared as strangers and asked for shelter, without being recognized. No one, therefore, should be so foolish as to risk showing

the door to a messenger sent by God. The Epistle to the Hebrews
could also have given a Christological basis for the obligation
of showing hospitality, as Jesus himself does in the parable of
the Last Judgment (Mt. 25:35). The author's choice of the
angels was probably inspired by the interest which his readers
seem to have had in the world of spirits (cf. Heb. 1-2).

The appeals which follow are directed against two vices which
are often mentioned in the same breath in the New Testament,
impurity and greed. The striking thing here is the author's
moderation and reasonableness. He does not demand absolute
continence or the radical renunciation of all possessions, as a
reaction against sinful behavior. His " ideal " of sexual purity is
a happy marriage; instead of choosing voluntary poverty, the
faithful must " be content with what is at hand," an attitude
which can include the cheerful and contented enjoyment of
earthly goods. Contentment and reliance on God sound like
bourgeois virtues, and it has sometimes been remarked rather
superciliously that the epistle here falls short of the severe norms
of the Sermon on the Mount. It is true that the church at the
end of the apostolic age had not always succeeded in maintaining the enthusiasm which characterized its early days. However,
it would be wrong to imagine that " bourgeois Christianity "
as it is called, which is found to a far greater extent in the
pastoral epistles, had abandoned any of the essential elements
of the gospel.

*Orthodoxy in the Faith, Courage in Suffering, True Worship, and
Obedience to the Church (13:7-17)*

⁷*Remember your leaders who addressed God's word to you.
Reflect on the outcome of their lives and imitate their faith.*

⁸Jesus Christ yesterday and today [is] the same for ever. ⁹Do not be led astray by all kinds of strange doctrines. [It is] good when a man's heart is confirmed by grace, not by different kinds of food. Those who live [like that] draw no benefit from them. ¹⁰We have an altar, and those who minister in the tent have no right to eat of it. ¹¹The bodies of the animals whose " blood was brought into the sanctuary as a sacrifice for sin" were "burned outside the camp" by the high priest (Lev. 16:27). ¹²Therefore Jesus, too, died outside the gate, to sanctify the people by his own blood. ¹³Let us, then, go out to him " outside the camp," bearing his shame. ¹⁴We have not here a city which remains; instead, we look for a city which is to come. ¹⁵Through him, we now wish to present an eternal sacrifice of praise to God, that is the fruit of lips which acknowledge his name. ¹⁶Do not forget to be active in doing good, sharing the same spirit. God is overjoyed with such sacrifices. ¹⁷Listen to your leaders and be at their disposal. They keep watch over your souls, because they must give an account. They must be able to do it joyfully, not with regret; this would be no advantage to you.

These verses are held together by references to the teaching authority of the leaders of the community, both dead (13:7) and alive (13:17). The connecting link, therefore, seems to be the need to hold fast to the true faith, as it was taught and is being taught by those who bear office in the church. It is true that when we descend to detail we meet appeals and motives which differ widely. It is questionable whether the author developed his principal theme logically, or merely allowed himself to digress under the influence of the association of ideas. Because of the obscurity of many of his statements, it seems advisable to limit ourselves to what is clear and unmistakable. Otherwise, the force of the passage would be lessened by hypotheses which are uncertain.

As is clear from numerous passages (cf. 2:3; 5:12; 6:10; 10:32–34), the community to which the Epistle to the Hebrews was addressed already had a long history behind it. Their first missionaries and superiors are described with a word which has a very profane sound: "leader," or "guide" (*hegoumenoi*; cf. Acts 15:22; 1 Clem. 1:3; 21:6). They were already dead. It is not clear whether they died as martyrs, but in any case they kept the "faith" to the end. Consequently, they were an example to the readers of the epistle. The context suggests that the idea of faith here involves more than mere steadfastness, as in previous passages. Here it seems to include orthodox and unadulterated doctrine. The sources for the late apostolic age show us that the most varied types of "heresies" were becoming widespread in the church. These involved speculative systems, together with various intuitions and practices, which are usually grouped together under the common name "Gnosticism." It would be surprising if such syncretistic influences were not to be found in the church to which the Epistle to the Hebrews is addressed. With a keen insight, the author sees what distinguishes orthodox faith from "all kinds of strange doctrines," namely, recognition of the fact that the historical Jesus and the pneumatic Christ are one and the same person. The Gnostics ignored the "Jesus of yesterday," and appealed exclusively to the secret revelations of the "Christ of today," the Lord of glory who now speaks through the Spirit. True faith, on the other hand, regards all that Jesus taught, did, and suffered in the past as the final revelation which has been given to us once and for all.

It is more difficult to say what the points of controversy which follow are concerned with. It may be that Christians who were influenced by these false teachings thought that a person could be " confirmed in his heart " by eating, or refusing to eat, certain foods. Prescriptions concerning food which are based on a particular view of the world are to be found in all ages and in almost every form of religion. Therefore, the reference need not necessarily be to the Jewish law of ritual purity; in gnostic circles, too, people abstained from certain foods, to avoid defiling their spiritual being by contact with matter which was evil (cf. 1 Tim. 4:3). On the other hand, certain foods were credited with the power of sustaining man's heavenly nature. Our epistle attacks this attitude very bluntly. A Christian is " confirmed in heart," not by eating certain foods, but by grace, the grace which comes from the cross of Christ alone. No one, therefore, can claim to be able to attain salvation by eating " sacred " food. Anyone who wants to make his way into " the city which is to come " must be prepared to share Christ's shame and leave this world.

However, it may be possible to throw a clearer light on the background of this controversy. As the reason for the uselessness of religious rites concerning food, the epistle gives a Christian interpretation of the Old Testament prescription that the bodies of the animals sacrificed on the great Day of Atonement had to be burned outside the camp. Therefore, the priests who " minister in the tent " did not partake of a sacrificial meal. The author seems to be trying to say that it is the same in the case of the Christian " altar." Here, too, there can be no sacrificial meal which would make a real participation in Christ's cross superfluous and guarantee eternal happiness by the mere eating of sacred food. We do not close our eyes to the great difficulties such an explanation involves. It almost looks as if the author denied the existence of the eucharistic meal, as if he considered Christian worship merely as a spiritual " sacrifice of praise," and as if he regarded " doing good and sharing a common spirit " as being superior to any liturgical rite. Before rejecting this " anti-sacramental "—or, better, " anti-sacramentalistic "—interpretation as unworthy of consideration, we should first think whether perhaps our modern eucharistic piety may not be subject to the same misunderstandings which the Epistle to the Hebrews condemns. Think, for instance, of the exaggerated importance attached to statistics concerning the reception of Holy Communion, of the way the service of the word is neglected, of the deep-seated misapprehension that attending Mass and receiving Holy Communion are more meritorious and of greater religious value than the practice of charity or really following Christ crucified.

Anyone who would criticize the church's rites and its attitude towards them today, as the author of the Epistle to the Hebrews does, must be prepared to incur the displeasure of the authorities. Modern preachers, theologians, and responsible lay persons who think with them, can therefore be confronted with a problem which certainly did not occur to our author when he formulated the exhortation: " Obey your leaders and be subject to them " (13:17). Must we give such unquestioning obedience to ecclesiastical authorities when they are really in the wrong? We believe that the obligation of obedience always remains, unless an ecclesiastical superior commands something sinful. But we also believe that the way in which genuine obedience is shown can no longer be modeled on the example of military or absolutist submission; these are now out of date. Where truth and right are concerned, there can be no question of a corpse-like obedience, or of submission of one's intellect. The obedience we owe the church authorities can never be dissociated from the obedience we owe to scripture, the gospel, and our own conscience. Ecclesiastical superiors have a grave pastoral duty for which they must one day " give an account." We can lighten this burden for them if we do our utmost to arrive at the most balanced possible knowledge of the truth, responsibly, prudently, and discreetly. We must not be discouraged by human failure to understand, or human narrowmindedness.

*Conclusion: A Request for Prayers, a Final Blessing, an
Exhortation, News of Timothy, and Farewell (13:18-25)*

¹⁸*Pray for us. We are convinced that we have a clear conscience, and we are always striving to live well.* ¹⁹*I admonish you to do this all the more, so that I may be given back to you sooner.* ²⁰*The God of peace brought the great Shepherd of the sheep, Jesus our Lord, out from the dead in the blood of an eternal covenant.* ²¹*May he prepare you to do his will in all that is good, and create in us what is pleasing to him, through Jesus Christ. To him [God] be glory for ever and ever. Amen.* ²²*But I implore you, brothers, to listen to these words of exhortation; for one thing, I have only written you a short letter.* ²³*Know that our brother Timothy has been set free. I will see you with him, if he comes soon.* ²⁴*Greet all your superiors and all the saints. Those who come from Italy greet you.* ²⁵*Grace be with you all.*

The author abandons his anonymity slightly in these concluding verses. However, he does not give us enough information to clear up the obscurity in which the circumstances surrounding the origin of the epistle are shrouded. The questions when, where, by whom, and to whom the letter was written are only of historical interest. Of greater interest for a commentary intended for spiritual reading are the assertions and instructions which have a bearing on our lives. The first of these is the author's request for the prayers of his readers or hearers. We know nothing of the particular reason for this request; the author may have been the object of hostility or suspicion, or he may have been in prison. In any case, he was anxious to see his correspondents soon again, and he wanted them to give him the help of their prayers. His request, therefore, was a genuinely human and personal one which, of course, does not mean that the community were not to pray for the spiritual progress, the " health of soul," of their pastor as well. The idea that the faithful are bound to pray for their apostles, missionaries, preachers, and teachers, is as old as the church itself. It is based on Jesus' prayer for his disciples. Apart from its immediate religious and practical significance, we believe that such prayerful communion between a community and its pastor could also contribute to a better understanding of the implications of an office in the church. A Christian priest is not merely an officially appointed [and paid] intercessor for his community, although this too is a duty which it would be impossible to take too seriously; he himself needs the prayers of the faithful, the " Pray, brethren," that his ministry may be pleasing to God. This dependence should preserve the clergy from presumptuousness and clerical arrogance.

The author now formulates a solemn prayer of intercession for the community, as a counterpart to his request for their prayers on his behalf. The text, which reaches its climax in a liturgical hymn of praise, once more recalls God's saving activity in overcoming death. The " God of peace " " brought the great Shepherd of the sheep out " from the world of the dead (cf. Is.

63 : 11–13). This image creates an almost overpowering impression; it reminds us of the high priest who is our " leader " and " precursor," a reference which is repeated in explicit terms in the phrase " in the blood of an eternal covenant." Here, for the first and only time in the whole epistle, the author mentions Jesus' resurrection. The object of his prayer in his formula of blessing also has a Pauline ring about it; that God might create in us what is good and pleasing in his sight. Therefore, we can " do God's will " (cf. 10 : 7.9.36) only if God " prepares " us. The Greek term here (*katartisai*) is the one used in 10 : 5 where, following a quotation from Psalm 40 (v. 7), the author speaks of God's " preparation " of Christ's body. There, too, " doing God's will " was the point at issue (10 : 7).

In his final appeal, the author begs his readers to bear, or to put up with, his sermon, the " words of exhortation " contained in his letter. As if by way of excuse, he adds that, after all, he has only written them a " short " letter (cf. in the opposite sense, 5 : 11!). It is certain that even in antiquity opinions were divided as to what was a long or a short sermon. For us, at least, the thirteen chapters of this epistle would be an unbearably long sermon, if they were all read at once. However, the point here is probably not so much the length of the epistle or its brevity. The author had not been sparing in his use of reproaches, rebukes, and threats. He must surely have had reason to fear that many members of the community whom he had especially in view would become indignant and perhaps reject the whole letter. Moreover, the letter also contained some very difficult ideas, as the author himself realized clearly (5 : 11). Therefore, " patience " and a real effort would be required to welcome the message of the epistle in a way which would bring fruit. This patient " bearing " or " putting up with " God's word (cf. Lk.

8:15) seems to have become quite a problem towards the end of the apostolic age. People were no longer willing " to bear sound teaching. Instead, they gathered great numbers of teachers according to their own tastes, to flatter their ears " (2 Tim. 4:3).

Are things any better today? Despite the biblical movement and the enthusiasm for scripture which is fashionable at the moment we, too, often lack the patience to let God's word of comfort, exhortation, and warning grow in us and reach maturity. Some people would like to interpret scripture almost *a priori*, and in a way which would be binding for all future generations. They shy from the effort and the risk involved in staking their life and death on God's " two-edged " word (cf. 4:12). Others proclaim their new discoveries day by day, as if they were the last word science had to say. They, too, refuse to wait until God himself reveals the secrets of his word to the human spirit as it prays and investigates with all humility. God shows great patience with us; he bears with us despite our weakness and our malice. Surely we, too, must have greater patience with his word which often seems so mysterious and strange to us.

The Epistle of St. James

INTRODUCTION

Practical Christianity

The Epistle of St. James occupies the first place among the group
of epistles known as the Catholic epistles, because it is the longest
of them all. With the exception of 2 and 3 John, these epistles
are not addressed to a particular person or local church; instead,
they are addressed to a number of Christians and are really sort
of encyclicals. Of all the "Catholic epistles," the Epistle of St.
James has the greatest right to this title; it is, in fact, an ethical
and religious treatise cast in the form of a letter. This is clear
from the lack, not only of any form of greetings or signature
at the end of the letter, but also of any perceptible relationship
between the writer and the addressees on a personal level. The
addressees were Jewish Christians of the diaspora who endured
poverty and oppression in their lives among the pagans of Syria
and Cilicia, as it seems.

The author introduces himself simply as "James, God's servant and the servant of our Lord Jesus Christ" (1:1). He makes
no effort to describe his authority more accurately; he obviously
takes it for granted that the recipients of his letter recognized it.
He, too, was a Christian of Jewish origin. He had a good knowledge of the Old Testament and was well acquainted with the
Jewish spirituality of his time. In addition, he enjoyed an
accurate insight into the needs of his fellow Christians, and he
wrote fluent Greek. Jerusalem at that time was bilingual, as was

Galilee, but it is not certain whether James " the Lord's brother " had such a good command of Greek; he may have used a Jewish Christian from the Greek diaspora to write the letter, as his secretary. James was the first head of the community at Jerusalem and St. Paul refers to him, together with Sts. Peter and John, as a " pillar " of the church (Gal. 2:9). If our supposition is correct, the letter dates from about A.D. 62-63 at the latest. It is an inspired document of apostolic times, as is guaranteed by its reception into the canon of sacred scripture, and as such its teaching is valid for the church in all ages.

The letter is constructed on the model of the " Wisdom books " of the Old Testament (Book of Proverbs, Ecclesiastes, Book of Wisdom, Ecclesiasticus). Exhortations, instructions, and practical norms for the everyday lives of Christians in the Jewish-Christian diaspora are loosely strung together in various groups of ideas. Besides Old Testament and Jewish ideas, the author consciously draws on the contemporary ethical and religious teaching of the earliest Christian tradition, as it was to be found in the primitive church at Jerusalem and in other Jewish-Christian churches. It is in this letter, for example, that we have the earliest written record of many of the sayings of the Sermon on the Mount. The characteristic demands of the supreme precept of charity also occupy a central place (2:8–11; cf. Mt. 22:39f.; Rom. 13:8–10).

Primarily, however, the letter's approach is determined by the spirit which governed Jesus' attitude. The ceremonial law of old has been abrogated. The new law to which Christians are subject is " the perfect law of freedom " (1:25; 2:12) which culminates in the " royal precept " of love for one's neighbor (2:8). The thought of any earthly reward as the motive for one's actions is completely excluded. The author's love and care are concentrated on the poor, and he has only hard words for those who are rich, with their wealth and their self-satisfied outlook (2:1-9; 4:13—5:6). "Has not God chosen those who are poor in this world to be rich in faith, to be heirs of the kingdom?" (2:5).

Humility (4:6.10), gentleness (1:20), mercifulness (2:13), love of peace (3:18), hospitality, interest in the poor (5:14), in sinners (5:16), and in those in need (4:15-17); the care of the sick, and even of those who have strayed and are lost (5:19f.), together with confident surrender to the providence of God our Father who arranges everything wisely and gives us only what is good for us (4:13-15; 5:7f.; 1:17)—these are the attitudes which must characterize and inspire a real Christian's life, according to the Epistle of St. James. Above all, however, a Christian must pray constantly and with perseverance, no matter what situation he may find himself in (1:6; 4:2-10; 5:13-18). He must persevere steadfastly in all the trials and difficulties of this life (1:3f.12; 5:7-12).

The Wisdom books of the Old Testament are content, by and large, to enunciate various rules of good sense and practical norms of conduct. The Epistle of St. James, on the other hand, is more interested in the complete submission of all spheres of a Christian's life to God's will, as it was revealed perfectly by Jesus Christ in all its depth. The author has only one great wish; this is, to ensure that the Jews who have become Christians take their faith seriously in their daily lives. The faith they have received and adopted as their rule of life must be translated into action. What is the use of an outwardly pious and God-fearing life, if its ultimate source and the goal at which it is directed are not inspired by faith? What use is a faith which does not bear fruit in a good life, or exercise any transforming influence? A faith which is not taken seriously in a person's daily life, or fails to have a decisive influence on his behavior, is unworthy of the name. It is an empty show. "The body without the soul is dead; so also faith without deeds is dead " (2:26).

St. James is not content merely to outline a general theory of the Christian life. He draws the conclusions and applies them inexorably to daily life. The phraseology he uses reflects in dramatic fashion the situation in which the Jewish-Christian churches of the diaspora found themselves, a situation which was obviously typical. Many of the Christians were poor and they were oppressed and exploited by wealthy landlords. They were even abused because of their faith and dragged into court (2:1–9; 5:1–6; 5:13). Consequently, many of them had fallen prey to a slavish hankering after anything which involved honor or authority, while they looked down on poorer Christians who were destitute or lacked education (2:1–8).

However, there were also wealthy Christians who were quite well-off. They allowed the others to pay them homage and they lived their lives according to their own plans with complete self-assurance, as if their fate were exclusively in their own hands (5:1–6; 4:13–17). There were others who had kind words for their brothers who were in need, but their hearts were hard, and they closed their purses and their hearts to their suffering. Envy and jealousy were rife, together with the self-righteous pursuit of "justice," accompanied by a critical attitude towards the behavior of other Christians or other human beings. Precipitate and overbearing remarks and judgments were common, as were calumny and detraction (4:1–12). Ill-humored grousing and grumbling threatened the spirit of unity among Christians (5:9a). There were some who were anxious to teach others, to exhort them, to instruct them, and to tell them what to do, but their enthusiasm was selfish. Consequently, it led to quarreling,

obstinacy, and hairsplitting; it even caused open conflicts and
jealousy (3:1—4:12). Discouragement in the face of the trials
and adversities of everyday life was widespread; they even
doubted God's loving providence, as if he were personally the
cause of everything that happened to his faithful in this world
(1:2-18).

It was no wonder that such behavior should lead to a half-
hearted faith, to lack of conviction in their prayer and in their
daily lives, and to hypocrisy and a sham piety (1:8.19-25; 2:14-
26; 4:1-17). In such circumstances, it was inevitable that the trials
they had to endure should become real temptations, which led
many Christians to fall (5:19f.). They had expected that Christ's
second coming as a Judge to reward them would be soon. When
this was delayed, it was no wonder that many of them should
have been tempted to make light of the judgment to come and
the end of all things, which Christians must prepare for. In their
selfishness and arrogance, they allowed themselves to be guided
by every conceivable type of passion and lived as people who
belonged to this world (4:13—5:11).

By way of contrast, St. James insists that God makes no distinction between man and man; he will test the faith of each
one and judge it by his deeds. Christ's coming is near and judgment has already been pronounced (5:1-9). St. James relentlessly
contrasts the behavior of these half-hearted Christians and their
readiness to compromise with Christ's demands. They must
take their faith seriously and live by it (1:8; 4:8). It is by his
fruits, by his daily life, that each one will be judged. Only a
practical Christianity will stand the test and win the promised
inheritance, when Christ comes again. This is an alert, a warning cry which is valid for the Christians of all ages; it is con-

stantly more and more necessary, and more and more actual. "Do you not realize that friendship with the world means enmity with God?" (4:4). Christians must prove themselves in the world by their whole-hearted and undivided faith and their unshakable confidence.

OUTLINE

The Opening of the Letter (1 : 1)

THE SENDER AND ADDRESSEES: GREETINGS (1 : 1)
  I. The sender (1 : 1a)
 II. The addressees; greetings (1 : 1b)

The Body of the Letter (1 : 2—5 : 20)

THE NATURE AND MEANING OF TEMPTATION (1 : 2-18)
  I. Temptation is a source of joy (1 : 2-4)
    1. It gives rise to steadfastness (1 : 2-3)
    2. Steadfastness leads to perfection (1 : 4)
 II. Wisdom is needed to realize this (1 : 5-8)
    1. Consequently, we must pray to God (1 : 5a)
    2. God gives without reservation or hesitation (1 : 5c)
    3. We must pray with faith and renounce all hesitation (1 : 6-8)
III. Appearances are deceptive (1 : 9-12)
    1. A Christian can boast only of his vocation (1 : 9-10a)
    2. Wealth does not last (1 : 10b-11)
    3. It is well for the man who can stand the test (1 : 12)
 IV. Only what is good comes from God (1 : 13-18)
    1. Our sinful lusts—the source of our temptations (1 : 13-15)
    2. God the author and source of all good (1 : 16-18)

HEARING AND PUTTING INTO PRACTICE (1 : 19-27)
  I. The correct attitude towards the message with which Christians are entrusted (1 : 19-21)

133

      1. Listen willingly (1 : 19–20)

      2. Welcome the " implanted word " submissively (1 : 21)

  II. Putting the word into practice properly (1 : 22–25)

      1. Be doers of the word (1 : 22–24)

      2. Salvation is promised only to those who do the word (1 : 25)

  III. The characteristic marks of genuine devoutness (1 : 26–27)

      1. Genuine devoutness not merely a matter of words (1 : 26)

      2. Genuine devoutness proves itself in love of one's neighbor and in sanctifying one's own life (1 : 27)

AN ATTACK ON PARTIALITY (2 : 1–13)

  I. The practice of the faith must be kept free of any partiality (2 : 1–7)

      1. Those who give preferential treatment to the rich do wrong (2 : 1–4)

      2. God has chosen the poor to be heirs of the kingdom (2 : 5–6a)

      3. The rich bear the chief responsibility for oppressing Christians (2 : 6b–7)

  II. Obey the royal law (2 : 8–13)

      1. The man who loves unselfishly does well (2 : 8)

      2. A person who acts partially incurs the guilt of sin (2 : 9–11)

  III. Follow the law of freedom (2 : 12–13)

FAITH AND WORKS (2 : 14–26)

  I. Faith without deeds is dead (2 : 14–19)

      1. Faith without deeds is unavailing (2 : 14)

      2. It is only by deeds that faith manifests itself (2 : 15–20)

  II. The testimony of sacred scripture (2 : 21–25)

1. Abraham was justified by his deeds (2:21-24)
2. Rahab was saved because of her deeds (2:25)
3. Summing up (2:26)

SINS OF THE TONGUE (3:1-12)

I. Do not be anxious to be teachers (3:1-2a)
II. Anyone who does not offend in speech is perfect (3:2b-4)
III. The destructive power of the tongue (3:5-8)
    1. A source of evil (3:5-6)
    2. Untamed power (3:7-8)
IV. A Christian's words should be words of praise and blessing (3:9-12)
    1. The sad reality (3:9-10a)
    2. The truth which is commanded (3:10b-12)

A CONDEMNATION OF THE SPIRIT OF THE WORLD,
OF JEALOUSY AND OF QUARRELING (3:13—4:12)

I. True and false wisdom (3:13-18)
    1. True wisdom is manifested by a good life (3:13)
    2. The source and the results of false wisdom (3:14-16)
    3. The source and the results of true wisdom (3:17-18)
II. Friendship with the " world " means enmity with God (4:1-6)
    1. The spirit of the world the source of all discord (4:1-3)
    2. God wants our whole selves (4:4-6)
III. Take your faith seriously (4:7-12)
    1. Therefore, you must be converted and return to God (4:7-10)
    2. Above all, do not judge (4:11-12)

A CONDEMNATION OF PRESUMPTUOUS SELF-ASSURANCE (4:13—5:6)

I. Woe to the self-assured (4:13-17)
    1. God alone disposes of the future (4:13-14)

    2. Presumptuous self-assurance is sinful (4 : 15–17)

II. Woe to the rich with their hard-heartedness (5 : 1–6)

    1. Sentence is already being passed (5 : 1–3)

    2. Injustice calls out to God for vengeance (5 : 4–6)

AN APPEAL FOR PATIENCE AND PERSEVERANCE (5 : 7–11)

  I. Wait patiently for the Lord's coming (5 : 7–9)

    1. Take heart, the Lord is near (5 : 7–8)

    2. Do not grumble against one another; the Judge is at the door (5 : 9)

  II. God will provide a happy ending (5 : 10–11)

    1. Follow the example of the prophets (5 : 10)

    2. It is well for the man who perseveres (5 : 11)

The Closing of the Letter (5 : 12–20)

CONCLUSION (5 : 12–20)

  I. Above all, do not take an oath (5 : 12)

  II. Pray in all the circumstances of your lives (5 : 13–18)

    1. In joy and sorrow (5 : 13)

    2. In sickness and in sin (5 : 14–18)

III. Have a care for your brother who has strayed (5 : 19–20)

THE OPENING OF THE LETTER
(1:1)

THE SENDER AND ADDRESSEES: GREETINGS
(1:1)

The Sender (1:1a)

^{1a}*James, God's servant and the servant of the Lord Jesus Christ . . .*

The Epistle of St. James is not really a letter. However, the author chose to adopt the form of a letter customary in antiquity. The introductory verse tells us first of all who wrote the letter and then to whom it was sent; it concludes with the usual introductory salutation *chairein*, " Greetings." The writer's name and the authority he enjoys are intended to lend weight and validity to what he has to say. Anyone who has a message for God's church must come in God's name and in the name of our Lord Jesus Christ, and by their authority. He must be commissioned by Christ, and his words must have the support of God's truth, if they are to be binding on God's people.

As an authorized " servant of the word " and " teacher " of the church (3:1), the writer appeals to the authority he enjoys. His authority is above suspicion; in contrast to the reasons usually given for the authority people enjoy in the world, it is not based on a show of rank or nobility. On the contrary, he describes himself as the slave, the servant, of a higher authority, God and his " Anointed " (Christ—Messiah); that is, Jesus, the risen Lord who sits at God's right hand. The title " slave " or

" servant " refers not only to the fact that the writer depends completely upon God and has been taken into his service; it also underlines the joy he feels at being chosen and commissioned in this way, at being " seized " by God and his Messiah as their possession. The privilege of being God's servant is a gift of grace and an honor. Even the Old Testament could think of no more honorable title for the great men of Israel than the title Servant. Consequently, this is the description we are given of Moses (Josh. 14:7), Joshuah (Josh. 24:29; Judg. 2:8), Abraham (Ps. 104:42), David (Ps. 88:4), Isaac (Deut. 3:35), and the Prophets (4 Kings 17:23); God made them his servants.

The same is true here. The only difference is that now God acts and has acted through his Anointed, the " Lord " Jesus. All those who acknowledge Jesus as the Lord and God's Anointed are God's servants and servants of Jesus Christ. As in the case of the great men of the Old Testament, this title underlines the realization that those who bear it have been taken into God's service in a special way and have received a special commission; they have been chosen out and given special authority. This is also true of St. Paul; he often refers to himself by this title in his writings. Unlike St. Paul, however, our author does not refer to his office as an apostle. He describes the authority he enjoys with the words " slave, servant, minister "—like the author of the Epistle of St. Jude, the " brother of James " (Jude 1). However, this simple description serves to remind the reader that the writer is speaking exclusively in the name of God and of the Lord Jesus Christ, and by their authority alone. Indeed, it is " the Lord " himself who speaks. What an extraordinary claim! And what a promise! In the writings of his servant, we meet the Lord, God's Anointed; we meet the hidden God himself. It is no wonder that such a document should be at pains to inculcate the need to observe God's will as the Lord Jesus revealed it, wholly and entirely.

The Addressees; Greetings (1:1b)

¹ᵇ. . . *to the twelve tribes in the diaspora:* [*Joyful*] *greetings!*

St. James here addresses his Christian correspondents with a term which was commonly used with reference to the twelve tribes of Israel who were scattered among the gentiles. After the destruction of the Northern Kingdom of Israel (722 B.C.) and the dispersal of the majority of the population of the Kingdom of Juda in the south (587 B.C.), a great part of the chosen people lived in the diaspora. One result of this was that many gentiles were won over to the worship of the one true God; another was that many members and even entire tribes of the chosen people were absorbed by their gentile host nations. From the days of the prophets, it had been the fervent hope of the Jewish people that, in the last stage of time, God would once more gather his people togther into one people of God and bring home those who were lost.

This is the only passage in the New Testament in which this expression is used. Its use implies a reference on St. James's part to his great namesake Jacob, the father of the twelve tribes. It means that the Messiah sent by God has already begun to gather together the lost members of God's people; the church is the true Israel. Therefore, he deliberately omits the word " Israel," the name of the people of God of old, from the address. St. James also implies that he himself is following in the footsteps of the patriarch Jacob. As head of the primitive church in Jerusalem he was provisionally responsible for the twelve tribes who had been discovered once more. These were the members of the chosen people who had received faith in the Messiah. However, they must first prove themselves in a world which is hostile to God (4:4–6), even though the day when God's people will be definitively brought home is already foreshadowed (5:1–11).

In speaking as he does, St. James realizes that he is an heir to Jesus' doctrine; he speaks on his behalf and on behalf of his " twelve," to whom was entrusted the task of bringing home God's people who were scattered throughout the world and lost. A promise had been made to them that they would rule over the twelve tribes of Israel. This has special reference, obviously, to those who, like St. James himself, belonged by blood to the descendants of the twelve sons of Jacob, although our author is well aware that the church which is made up of Jews *and* gentiles now constitutes the true Israel. He sends his joyful greetings, therefore, to all these brothers of his and to all those who belong to the true Israel; and this includes us.

THE BODY OF THE LETTER
(1:2—5:20)

THE NATURE AND MEANING OF
TEMPTATION (1:2–18)

St. James immediately takes up his first train of thought, which deals with temptation. The principal ideas and terms he uses occur again and again, and further themes are attached directly to this train of thought without any introduction. The " themes " he deals with arise spontaneously from the situation he has in mind. In each case, he underlines the proper Christian attitude and shows up clearly and without mincing his words the unsatisfactory behavior Christians were guilty of in practice. The pious fraud that merely believing in Christianity was sufficient to make a person a Christian and bring him to salvation must be completely excluded. Genuine faith must prove itself in a person's daily life if it is to be effective for salvation.

Temptation is a Source of Joy (1:2–4)

It Gives Rise to Steadfastness (1:2–3)

²*Regard it as an unalloyed joy, my brothers, when you fall into temptations of every kind.* ³*You know, certainly, that the testing of your faith inspires steadfastness.*

Resuming an idea implied in his greeting, St. James takes up the key-word " joy " once more and applies it to temptation. In every respect, temptation, the testing of one's faith, is a cause of rejoicing. This is a daring and even a shocking statement,

145

when we remember the sinister and dangerous reality concealed in the idea of temptation. For anyone who believes in the providence of a good and holy God who is our Father in heaven, this word contains a frightful mystery. Such a person must constantly experience the realization that even good and loyal Christians are exposed in many ways to the power of the Tempter, even to the extent of being cast into the depths of despair, of mute apostasy, or betrayal. The dark shadow of temptation stretches from our first parents (Gen. 3:1-19) over Abraham, the father of all faith (Gen. 22:1-19), and the innocent Job, to Jesus in the desert (Mt. 4:1-11) and on the Mount of Olives (Mk. 14:32-42). It reaches beyond Judas, Thomas, and the apostles, to the end of the world. That is why, in the sixth petition of the Our Father (Mt. 6:13; Lk. 11:4), Jesus teaches us to pray that we may be kept safe from temptation. He warns us to be on our guard constantly and to pray for God's protection when we are tempted (Mk. 14:38).

On the other hand, it is only where faith exists that it can be assailed. It is only in temptation that faith can prove itself as a form of complete submission to God's will. We are told this even in the Old Testament. "My son, if you have made up your mind to serve God, be prepared for temptations. At the same time, you must have courage and persevere, and not act rashly in the time of trial. Cling to God and do not fall away from him; then you will be exalted, when it is all over. Accept whatever comes your way and be patient in the ups and downs of tribulation. God is proved by fire; the man who is pleasing to God is proved in the furnace of affliction " (Sir. 2:1-5). It is this which enables St. James to conclude quite simply that the testing of a person's faith inspires steadfastness. Temptation is the very means by which Christians are put to the proof. This is the basic attitude which the Christian who is afflicted in this world must have. Often enough, his trials will come from the members of his own people who have not the faith. To bear perfect fruit, a man must preserve his faith steadfast in all adversities. If he succeeds in doing that, he has reason to be joyful.

Steadfastness Leads to Perfection (1:4)

⁴Steadfastness must result in a perfect work, so that you may be perfect and blameless, lacking nothing in any respect.

Faith must leave its imprint on every domain of a person's life, resolutely and systematically. A man's whole being and everything he does must be completely adapted to God's will. It is only then that God's saving design is accomplished; this is, to bring to perfection all those who have been redeemed. The Christian who has been redeemed must be perfect, free from stain, and lacking nothing; he must be perfect like his Father in heaven (Mt. 5:48). For St. James, the " perfect work " is not just some particular action or an individual virtue; it is the Christian himself in his mature and tested faith. This shows us how well St. James had understood his Lord. We should note, too, how subtly the construction of the sentence underlines the fact that this maturing process does not necessarily lead to the " perfect work " without more ado or automatically. Constant effort is needed, if the likeness of God his Father is to shine out in the Christian he has chosen. Here, too, St. James rules out any form of pious self-satisfaction. It is only where this perfections lacks nothing that faith is genuine; it is only then that faith has achieved its purpose. It is not enough to avoid this or that, or do this or that. God is determined that the whole man should be completely refashioned and brought to perfection.

Anyone who realizes how much he lacks and how poor he is, largely through his own fault, will be glad that his faith is being tried. Anyone who keeps the purpose of temptation in view and accepts it in his heart in a spirit of faith is bound to rejoice; there is no other way to reach the goal.

Wisdom is Needed to Realize This (1 : 5–8)

Consequently, We Must Pray to God (1 : 5a)

5a*If anyone among you lacks wisdom, he must pray for it to God . . .*

A proper grasp of the doctrine just expounded calls for the God-given gift of understanding. Living by faith means looking at life and the world with God's eyes; it means judging them by his standards. True wisdom, therefore, can come only from above (3 : 15). It often happens that a person's behavior in his daily life is in complete contradiction to the faith he professes. The reason is because faith did not lead to a change of outlook. Unless a person is prepared to change his outlook and accept God as the beginning and the end of all things, of all his plans, his decisions, and his activities, and judge everything in this light, his faith remains inadequate and bears no fruit. Such a person has not reached maturity; indeed, he still bears the stamp of the "wisdom of this world" which is completely taken up with the things of this world and leads to death (3 : 13–18).

Everything depends on this ability to see things in the light of God. Consequently, Christians must pray, and the more anxious a person is to be perfect and have a mature faith, the more fervently he must pray. In saying this, St. James was merely impressing upon his readers something with which they had long been familiar from their reading of the Old Testament, especially the Wisdom literature (cf. Prov. 2:3–6). They also had the example of Solomon who was renowned for his wisdom. When he made his request of God, it was not for a long life, or riches, or victory over his enemies; instead, he asked for the most precious gift God has to give, a wise, enlightened, and understanding heart which would be capable of distinguishing between good and evil (3 Kings 3:5–14). Unless a person prays perseveringly for this gift which is the basis of all other gifts, he will never be able to bring his faith to its full development. He will not have the right outlook.

How is it that we pray so little and so ineffectively for the gift of wisdom, a faith that is really enlightened? Is it because we have so little interest in having a perfect faith? Or because we doubt whether we could ever attain such a state of perfection? Perhaps it is because we doubt whether God would hear our prayers.

God Gives Without Reservation or Hesitation (1:5b)

⁵ᵇ . . . *who gives to all openly and without the slightest hesitation* . . .

Unlike a human being who is approached for help, God gives in a divine way. He does not resort to excuses or make reservations;

with him, there are no ifs or buts. He does not stop to consider whether the petitioner deserves a hearing or to have his prayer granted, or under what conditions it can be done most advantageously. He gives generously, without making mental reservations or voicing suspicion. He does this precisely because he is God, the giver of all good (1 : 17). He gives without grumbling about the petition, without making his supplicant feel he is unwilling to give, or implying that the answer to his request involves great condescension on his part. God gives gladly, with willing kindness. This, in turn, means that prayer is not something unwelcome; it is not an unpleasant chore or something dishonorable. It is something joyful and honorable. God bestows his gifts like a loving father on his child who prays to him. We know that children delight in going to their father with their requests, whether great or small. What is there to prevent us, then, from praying for wisdom?

⁵ᶜ . . . *and it will be given to him.*

It is certain that God will hear such a prayer. St. James does not merely state this. He has a witness to prove what he says, because he quotes Jesus his Lord. With this turn of phrase, St. James resumes an expression used in the Sermon on the Mount. It is an appeal to Christians to pray with confidence and a guarantee that such prayer will be heard (Mt. 7 : 7; Lk. 11 : 9). It is very significant that St. Luke tells us that the great gift God gives in answer to trusting prayer is the gift of his spirit, God's own gracious and sanctifying spirit. " If you who are evil know how to give good gifts to your children, how much more readily will not the heavenly Father give his holy spirit to those who pray to him for it " (Lk. 11 : 13). This is exactly what St. James means

when he tells us that we must pray for the gift of wisdom. If a
person is determined to win a share in God's perfection and fullness of life, surely there is nothing he needs more than the gift of
this transforming, sanctifying, and enlightening spirit? This
gives us a norm by which we can judge what we should pray
for, and it also tells us how we can be sure we will be heard.

We Must Pray with Faith and Renounce All Hesitation (1:6–8)

⁶ᵃ*However, he must pray in faith, without the slightest hesitation.*

To pray properly, it is not enough that a person should know
what he is praying for; he must also have firm confidence, based
on faith. If his prayer is to win a hearing, the person who prays
has a very important contribution to make. This is his un-
limited faith in God's goodness and love. A Christian's faith is
a bridge which leads to God's heart. The man who doubts
God's goodness, his fatherly care, or his willingness to grant our
prayers, calls all that Christ said and did into doubt. He reduces
God to the level of a fickle human being who cannot be depended upon; he breaks the bridge which is built on faith.
Hesitation of any kind prejudices trusting prayer. The apparently inevitable order of the universe, the raucous, fretful activity
of the world and of men, and even God's frequently incomprehensible silence may all speak against the power of trusting
prayer. Yet, if a man believes and does not hesitate, his prayer
has the power even to move mountains (Mt. 21:21). We have
Christ's word for it, and all power has been given to him. We
can rely with absolute certainty on his promise.

6b. . . . a person who hesitates is like a wave in the sea which is whipped by the wind and driven this way and that.

That is the position of a person who hesitates. He is tortured by the slightest breath of doubt. He is driven here and there and tossed about aimlessly by a variety of theories and opinions, with no principle, nothing he can hold fast to. He is empty, treacherous foam. This is a frightening picture of a Christian who should be firmly anchored in God. He is influenced more by the slightest whisper of an opinion than by God's firm and unshakable truth. In this passage, St. James is not talking about the genuine hesitation of a person who is suffering some affliction. What he has in mind is the half-heartedness and the emptiness of those who only " last for a moment." They are carried away by the first harsh gust of wind. In the words of our Lord's own parable, they are withered by the first rays of the burning sun, because they have no root (Lk. 8 : 13).

7Such a person must not expect to receive anything from the Lord; 8he is in two minds, inconstant in all his ways.

The promise that prayer offered in faith will infallibly be heard does not hold in the case of a Christian who has not got " unqualified " faith. Such a person can expect nothing from God. He himself has given nothing; he has not given God his confidence, and he does not give himself to him completely and without reservation. Consequently, he remains alone and enjoys no certainty. A person who is in two minds and does not trust God cannot afford to trust himself either. He is capable of nothing. He is torn between trust and distrust, between trust in God and trust in himself, between self-surrender and flight, between prayer and doubt, between finding and seeking, between hope and fear. Such a way of life is bound to be aimless and devoid of purpose. It is a pointless wandering to and fro which leads nowhere and is impossible to keep track of.

This passage makes it clear what faith means. It means giving oneself completely to God with implicit trust, and building one's whole life on this firm foundation. The man who refuses to commit himself to God without reservation, or who is not convinced of God's goodness and love, has nothing to which he can hold fast in all his activity. It is only when a Christian prays in a spirit of faith for the gift of wisdom, God's spirit and grace, that his faith can reach its full development.

The Christianity we meet in St. James is basic Christianity. His doctrine is authoritative and, if a person listens to him, he will be able to make the transition from half-heartedness and indecision to joyful, integral faith, such as is capable of vanquishing the world.

Appearances are Deceptive (1:9–12)

A Christian Can Boast Only of His Vocation (1:9–10a)

⁹*Let the brother who is in humble circumstances boast of his exaltation;* ¹⁰ᵃ*let the rich man, on the other hand, boast of his lowliness . . .*

At first sight, it seems that St. James now goes on to speak about boasting, without any introduction. In reality, however, he merely continues the train of thought he had already begun under a new aspect. A man's worth does not consist in the earthly goods he possesses; it consists in everything which makes him rich in God's eyes. Only what is of value in God's eyes is of any importance; nothing else is lasting. As a result of God's intervention in the world there has been a reversal of values. It is no longer man or his life here on earth which occupies the center of the stage; it is God and his gifts. It is only the man who is perfect in God's eyes that can afford to boast. Even then, he cannot boast of his own achievements, but only on the basis of the gift of grace he has received by God's unmerited favor. This is why we should be glad even over the difficulties we endure; they purify our faith like gold in the furnace.

The author develops his idea of a man's true worth with the help of two considerations which seem quite contradictory. In this he is in complete harmony with tradition; he does not rely solely on his own conviction. This approach is very common both in the Old and in the New Testament. " This is what the Lord says: Let not the wise man boast of his wisdom. Let not the man who is strong boast of his strength, or the man who is rich of his wealth. No, if anyone wants to boast, let him boast that he is wise enough to acknowledge me and to realize that I am the Lord who shows favor and exercises right and justice on the earth. It is in such persons I take pleasure " (Jer. 9:22f.). Jesus Sirach develops this thought: " The fear of the Lord is the only thing which the rich and the well-to-do can boast of, and the poor as well " (Sir. 10:21). The principle that a human being can make a well-founded boast only if he fixes his eyes on God, forgetting himself, and boasts of the grace God has shown in choosing him, is brought to its logical conclusion by St. Paul who gives us the classic formula: " If a man is determined to boast, let him boast in God " (1 Cor. 1:31). In Christ, God has removed all grounds for boasting, both from the gentiles and from the Jews; no one was to have any ground for boasting in his sight (I Cor. 1:25–31). A Christian, therefore, can boast only of Christ's love and his saving activity; it is this which has made him rich in God's eyes (Phil. 3:3). He should boast only of the benefits he receives as a result of sharing in his Lord's life, and especially of his share in Christ's powerlessness and suffering.

St. James underlines the " exaltation " and the " glory " a poor Christian can boast of, even though he may often be despised. He reminds rich and highly-placed Christians, on the other hand, that they should be humble and not forget that their true excellence also consists exclusively in the vocation they have received, in the fact that they are Christians. The epigrammatic formula, " Let the rich (brother) boast of his lowliness," is intended not merely as an exhortation to practice humility and boast in God alone, putting aside all pride and self-satisfaction; it is also meant as an indication of the dangers arising from wealth, which can so easily obscure a Christian's gaze and deceive him (cf. 4:13–16).

Wealth Does Not Last (1:10b–11)

10b. . . *because he will pass like " the bloom on the grass." *11*Once the sun rises with its heat, " the grass " is burned and its " bloom withers," and the beauty of its appearance is no more. So, too, the rich man will fade away, with all his enterprises.*

St. James applies the words of the Prophet Isaiah (Is. 40:6f.) to the rich man's fate. All the luster and splendor of wealth is inevitably doomed to disappear—like everything else in this world. The beauty of the lush pasture-land and the steppes of

Palestine after the seasonal rains vanishes in an incredibly short time. Of all the majesty of this world nothing is permanent. That is why the rich are poor; they allow themselves to be blinded and held captive by the glitter of something which cannot last and which leads to bitter deception. Even if a man had all the means in the world at his disposal, he could not arrest the decline of his vital powers. Consequently, the rich are doubly poor; not only are they wretched, they are also deceived in their hopes for life. Nothing is permanent, the whole world passes away. Only God is eternal, God and those who abandon themselves to him and place all their hope in him. They are rich in his eyes, through him, and in him.

Nowadays we realize more vividly than ever how timelessly valid and actual this cry of warning is for all those who call themselves Christians. They boast that they view things in their proper perspective, and they are aware of God's promises. It is urgently necessary that we should compare our standards, our hopes, and our expectations with this standard, the only one which is valid: He alone is rich who is rich in God's eyes.

It is Well for the Man Who Can Stand the Test (1:12)

[12]*It is well for the man who stands fast in temptation. Once he has proved himself, he will receive the crown of life which God has promised to those who love him.*

In this verse, the author once more resumes his opening theme (1:2–4). He sums up all that he has said so far in the form of a beatitude. In God's eyes, it is well for the man who has proved himself in the various hardships and difficulties he encounters because of his faith. The prize of victory which God has promised to all those who prove their worth in the struggle of life beckons him. The image of a crown of victory, which occurs frequently in the New Testament, is taken from the world of athletics. Faith does not preserve a man from the difficulties of life. On the contrary, it leads him straight into the thick of the struggle against forces which are hostile to God. At the same time, however, it enables a man to prove his worth in this contest. Here, too, St. James applies the teaching of his Master to the daily lives of Christians. " It is well for you when they insult you and persecute you and speak all kinds of evil against you untruly, for my sake " (Mt. 5 : 11).

A great reward awaits the man who has proved himself in this way—the fullness of God's life. " The man who has no part in the battle will not bear away the crown of eternal life." Therefore, a Christian really has cause to rejoice and praise God even here in this life, in the midst of all his trials. The man who endures trials and stands firm is assured of this reward, which is life itself. Yet it would be a serious misunderstanding to conclude from the fact that a Christian looks forward to a reward to come that he is merely an egoist of a more refined type. He is interested in a reward, even though it is a future, heavenly, reward. However, it is not for the sake of the reward or of his own advantage that a Christian remains true to his Lord in his daily life; it is for God's sake. It is God who has given him a place in his battle; it is God who has invited him to prove his worth. It was God who gave him his love first, and offered him a share in his own life as his inheritance, out of love alone. Love for God is the Christian's real driving force in the struggle of life.

" Your love, your will, your kingdom, your life "—that is the

Christian's battle-cry, because it was the rule of life of his Lord, Jesus Christ. A share in God's gracious reward, the crown of victory, is only for those who love God, not with pious words or with their lips alone, but with their whole lives. This is no wonder, when we remember that the content of the promised reward is described as a union of life and love with the God who condescends so graciously to men. For St. James, loving God means constantly proving oneself worthy of God's choice in one's daily life. This is a realistic approach. It makes it impossible to reduce the commandment of love to a matter of pleasant feelings or a purely interior attitude, if our love for God is to be genuine.

Only What is Good Comes from God (1:13–18)

Our Sinful Lusts—the Source of Our Temptations (1:13–15)

¹³*Let no one who is tempted say: " I am being tempted by God." God cannot be tempted to evil, and he himself tempts no one.*

May we not object that, if it is God's plan that temptations should help to test us and bring us to perfection, then God himself must surely be responsible for all those who fail in time of temptation, and so make shipwreck of their faith? Human beings have always been tempted to make God answerable for the evil which is to be found in the world and in their own lives, in the hope of reducing their own responsibility to the minimum. " It was the woman you gave me that led me into sin," Adam told God (Gen. 3: 12). The big argument is, of course, that God uses the evil, the sin, and the guilt which springs from man, and even Satan's influence, to further his own designs. In this way, he puts everything to good use. Joseph realized this when he acknowledged gratefully in the presence of his brothers: " You certainly meant harm, but God has brought good from it " (Gen. 50:20).

St. James first lays down the unshakable principle: God is not responsible for tempting anyone to sin. God's being is absolutely good, and he is incapable of tempting anyone. God is so good that he cannot intend anything which is evil in itself, or even less good, or enlist it in his service. Indeed, he is the source of all good, the Lord and Keeper of those who are good, on whom he bestows his rewards, while he avenges himself on the wicked. God is holy and he cannot be the cause of any temptation to evil. His whole desire is to ensure that " Everything should help to promote the well-being of those who love God " (Rom. 8:28), as St. Paul says so well.

St. James is conscious that he has " scripture " on his side here too. Sirach, for example, says: " Do not say, My sin comes from God. God is not responsible for something he hates. Do not say either, It was he himself who made me fall. It should not be that sinners should even exist. The Lord hates what is evil and outrageous, and he does not let it happen to those who fear him. The Lord created man in the beginning and left him to his own devices. If you want to, you can keep the commandments. All you need is the fidelity to do his will . . . God never gave man a commandment to commit sin, and he does not lend his support to people who are deceitful " (Sir. 15:11–20). The responsibility, therefore, is not God's.

But how is it, then, that our Lord could teach us to pray, in the Our Father, " Lead us not into temptation " (Mt. 6:13; Lk. 11:4), if God " tempts no one "? This objection is beside the point. The second part of the petition reads, ". . . but deliver us from the Evil One " (Mt. 6: 13). This shows that what we are really asking for is to be preserved from anything which could lead us into sin. What this petition means is, " Do not let us fall into temptation," that is, into any temptation which would exceed our strength, so that God knows we would give in to it. Jesus says quite clearly that God, who alone is good, holy, and perfect, can and does give only what is good, even to those who are evil. Indeed, God went so far as to send his Son to save sinners and seek out those who were lost, and reconcile them with his love. How could such a God entice us to sin and cast us into ruin?

[14]*On the contrary, each one is allured and enticed by his own lusts, and so he falls into temptation.* [15]*Once lust has conceived, it brings forth sin, and sin, once it reaches its term, gives birth to death.*

Man's downfall finds its roots in man himself, and not in God. In the midst of all his striving and all his desires, in the midst of his deepest urges, his lusts impel him towards sin. Man himself is inclined towards evil. St. James does not go any further into the question how it is that a creature which God made good should have an inclination towards evil; that he should have a real urge to rebel against God's will and a lust for all that runs counter to God's spirit, God's will. He simply presupposes that the world and the human race are wicked, that they are under the yoke of sin and the devil, and have become corrupt.

He is far more interested in opening the eyes of those who have been saved by Christ, and warning them against any dishonorable compromise, any public or private pact with the world of evil. The world of evil has been overcome, but it is still dangerous. That is why he shows, briefly and to the point, what happens when a person yields to temptation and where it leads. He compares a person's lusts to a prostitute or a courtesan who ensnares a guileless young man with her charms and traps him, until she enfolds him in her deadly embrace. The logical and sure consequence of this can only be eternal perdition. This comparison was familiar to readers of the Old Testament (cf. Prov. 7: 1–27). The words " entice " and " allure " also imply a reference to hunting. There a dumb animal is robbed of its caution by means of a bait which seems to offer it some gratification. It is forced to pay for this brief pleasure with its freedom and eventually with its life.

Man's fate, therefore, is in his own hands. From the outset, however, his will is disposed towards evil. Temptation comes from his own heart which is in bond to sin. Everything depends, therefore, on the attitude a man takes towards this slight inclination from the beginning. Anyone who does not say a decided No to his evil inclinations from the outset is already lost. This is particularly true if a person plays with the temptation or tries to place the responsibility for his temptation and his sins on God. Then one thing leads inevitably to another, temptation—sin—death. By the time such a person opens his eyes, it is too late. The sequence *lust—temptation—sin—death* places this fearful process, which is the experience of every sinner, forcibly before our eyes. It is an appeal to resist whole-heartedly and stand the test courageously, when we are tempted.

God the Author and Source of All Good (1:16–18)

[16]*Do not fool yourselves, my beloved brothers.* [17]*Only a gift which is good, an endowment which is perfect, can come from*

*above, from the Father of the [heavenly] lights, with whom
there is no change or darkening, such as results from the movement [of the stars].*

St. James now adduces a further argument against the theory
which holds that God is ultimately responsible for temptation
and sin. His argument this time is taken from creation, and his
approach is based on ideas which were common especially in the
world in which his readers lived. As the one who created the
world and conserves it, God is its Father. To illustrate what he
means, St. James chooses the stars as a case in point. The night
sky in the Orient is far brighter than in the West; consequently,
Easterners are far more conscious of the brilliance of the stars
than Westerners. God created these heavenly bodies in all their
glory, to fix the divisions of time and light the darkness. It is
he who gave them their well-ordered course and now he guides
them (cf. Gen. 1 : 14–19). He himself, however, is subject to no
earthly order or law of motion; he is immutable in his being
and in his activity. It is impossible that the divine Being which
is so good and so pure should be the cause of evil or of anything
imperfect. The gifts and endowments God gives are good, without exception, and they make those who receive them rich in
every good. Anyone who cannot see this is merely deceiving
himself in a serious matter. Such self-deception weakens a man,
when he is tempted, with disastrous consequences.

[18]*In accordance with his own design, he gave us birth through
the message of truth, so that we might be, in a certain sense, the
firstfruits of his creation.*

St. James has an even stronger argument against the false and
dangerous opinion which he wishes to refute. By his own free

will, God determined to save us, his poor creatures, even though we were sinners. How could he now contradict his own decision, his own achievement, by tempting those who were redeemed, and so lead them into sin once more? No, God's will is unchanging, and his will is that we should be saved. There is no reason whatever to doubt the saving love of God our Father, even in time of temptation. Then his support is the only thing we can cling fast to, the only sure reason we have for being confident of our ability to withstand all temptations victoriously.

God accomplishes our salvation by means of the message of truth. When a person accepts the message of faith preached by God's church concerning the salvation which he offers the lost world in Jesus Christ, God makes him his child. He takes him into his family and gives him a share in his own life. It is by welcoming the message of salvation preached by the church in a spirit of faith that we are saved. St. James underlines this by choosing an unusual word to describe God's saving activity: *apokyein,* to give birth to. The " message of truth " is compared to the maternal agent by means of which God " brings to birth " those who accept his salvation. He gives them new life, which is the only true life. St. James is not thinking here of the sacrament of baptism, which he does not mention. What he has in mind is the message of faith which is the source of our salvation, the " message of truth." Baptism, then, is the effective accomplishment of the re-birth which comes to us through the message of truth, when we welcome it in a spirit of faith. It puts the final seal on our re-birth.

St. James also mentions the goal of this renewal. Those who have been born anew are to be the firstfruits, a pledge of the future renewal of all creation. It is clear that two trains of thought are involved in this formula. God prepares choice and perfect gifts for himself from the world of creation, just as human beings offer up choice fruits in sacrifice. God takes pleasure in such firstfruits and he accepts them willingly. At the same time, however, those who have already been born anew have a representative function to perform. They are a testimony to the fact that the final renewal of the whole world has already begun in germ in the church. This renewal is aimed at the transformation of all humanity and even of the entire universe. The new world has already been inaugurated in those who are God's children; the final transformation of the cosmos cannot be long delayed. With Christ, the last stage of time has already begun (cf. 5 : 7–9).

St. James says, " So that we might be . . ." He is overjoyed at the thought that God has made him, and us too, his children, by giving us new birth, so that we are the firstfruits of his new universe. In those who already enjoy " re-birth," God has given the world a sign which entitles it to hope for the redemption of the whole universe. Besides the joy this gives him, St. James also recalls the dignity and the duties it involves for those who have been born anew. The " message of truth," the faith, is meant to be lived. The new being a Christian receives must show itself in a new life. Consequently, St. James is not content to leave it at that, even though this statement forms the climax of the first section of his letter; God has given us new birth and we are his children, the firstfruits of the redeemed world. Instead, he uses this truth as the starting point for what follows; how must those who have been born anew live, so that what God has already achieved may produce its effect and reach its full development? God's activity demands man's coöperation in attaining the goal God has set, the " perfect work " which is the new man in God's kingdom (1 : 4).

HEARING AND PUTTING INTO PRACTICE
(1:19-27)

A new train of thought follows which is devoted to another trait which is characteristic of genuine Christianity. The faith which Christians know and profess, of its very nature, demands to be put into practice if it is to be genuine. Consequently, in the very middle of the passage, we have the demand that Christians should be doers, and not merely hearers; they should be " doers of the word " (1:22.23), " active doers " (1:25). Any faith which is confined to the realm of the intellect is merely a pious fraud. That is why St. James makes a point of citing various examples of practical faith in conclusion; the selfless care of those in need (1:27: widows and orphans) and the struggle to lead a life pleasing to God.

The Correct Attitude Towards the Message with which Christians are Entrusted (1:19-21)

Listen Willingly (1:19-20)

[19]*You know this, my beloved brothers; a man should be quick [willing] to listen, but slow to speak, slow to anger.* [20]*Man's anger does not promote the justice which comes from God.*

The solemn form of address, with the introductory phrase, " You know," underlines a Christian's responsibility towards the message of truth. The correct attitude to be adopted is outlined in three phrases which are reminiscent of the Wisdom literature. A Christian must be ready and open to receive any word coming from another; he must listen patiently and lovingly. It is in listening that we encounter both our fellow men and God as other persons. That is why a Christian must have a spirit of reverence and refuse to shut his heart, when God or his fellow men address him or make some claim upon him. Only a person who knows how to listen is capable of understanding; only a person who listens willingly and reverently can give a true, loving, and sympathetic answer. This is true especially when it is God who speaks or makes some claim on a man : " He who has ears to hear, let him hear!" (Mk. 4:9). St. James is particularly anxious that his readers should display this willingness to listen, especially to God's word; they must listen willingly to the preaching of the faith, and during divine worship. This is clear from the way this general norm is applied in the following verses. Every Christian must have the right attitude towards the message of truth; he must practice the art of listening, if he is to be capable of a genuine encounter with God's word.

St. James also emphasizes a Christian's responsibility towards his own words; he must be " slow to speak." A man is responsible for every word he says. In a subsequent passage, our author deals in greater detail with the really diabolical power man enjoys (3:1-12). At the moment, he is interested only in laying down the supreme norm of all speech and behavior—what is right in God's eyes. This is the meaning of the reference to God's justice, that characteristic gift which is bestowed as of right on those who try to allow God's will its full scope in their lives.

In the struggle to win the gift of justice, the proper control of one's own words is of decisive importance. It is not merely a matter of avoiding thoughtless gossip, or rash judgments or remarks. Ultimately, what is important is the attitude by which a person's words are inspired. Are they inspired by a reverent, objective, and discreet openness based on truth and love, or by a self-centered, vain, assertive, touchy, vindictive, and uncontrolled impulsiveness, such as is typical of the spirit of the world (cf. 3:13—4:12)? When hate, anger, revolt, or that pride which sets itself up as a god gains control of a man, his words are endowed with diabolical possibilities. We have an example of this in the appalling insults and blasphemies uttered by Jesus' enemies as they stood beneath his cross (Mt. 27:39-44). Irresponsible words which are not inspired by truth or love are ultimately bound to destroy the person who speaks them. The time will come when God will demand from everyone an account of every word he has spoken (Mt. 12:36).

Welcome the "Implanted Word" Submissively (1:21)

²¹*Lay aside, therefore, all defilement, your overflowing wickedness, and grasp the word implanted in you with all submissiveness; it has power to save your souls.*

It is not enough, however, to avoid sins of speech, or sins committed against God's word; malice and wickedness of all kinds must be renounced and put away. We can be sure St. James is thinking here of baptism. Baptism does away with all defilement and sinfulness of every kind and clothes the person who receives it in the holiness which belongs to his Lord. Christians, therefore, already enjoy freedom from sin and imperfection in principle, but this must now find expression in their lives. It must be demonstrated particularly by the rejection of all kinds of wickedness and sinfulness, which are a constant threat to the new life Christians have received.

By the implanted word St. James means the teaching of the faith as a formulated doctrine, and also the profession of faith made by those who were to be baptized. This word which is implanted in the faithful is constantly nourished by the church's teaching, and it must produce plentiful fruit in the life of every baptized Christian. However, its power to produce fruit depends not only on its own efficacy, but also on the coöperation of the faithful. In contrast to man's anger, which St. James has already condemned, a Christian coöperates properly with God's word by submissiveness, by adopting an attitude of gentle and humble affability which places all its trust in God.

In this, we have Christ's own example. We must follow the example of his attitude towards the will of his Father in heaven and towards his fellow men, who were in such need of redemption. The beatitude he pronounced concerning those who are gentle must give us strength (Mt. 5:5). God's kingdom has been promised as an inheritance to those who depend upon God for everything and upon themselves for nothing, and accept God's offer of salvation and persevere in it, in a spirit of joy and trust. St. James's teaching continues that of Jesus. The people he addresses are the same poor, ordinary, humble people who were so much in need of salvation, to whom Jesus originally addressed his message. In St. James's letter, we meet the attitude of poverty, humility, tenacity, meekness, and joy which is characteristic of a submissive spirit. In this, too, he is an heir to Christ's teaching which he proclaims anew with all his apostolic authority. It is significant that he once more emphasizes the need to put the message of faith, with the claims it makes, into practice: " Grasp the word implanted in you." Be constantly occupied with this.

Live by this new life, this vital power! Let this efficacious leaven produce its effect on all your thoughts and desires. Reform your lives in keeping with it. This is a basic program which can only be put into effect properly by means of constant dialogue with God's word, as it is proclaimed and taught to us. " Living by the word " is as much a mark of genuine Christianity today as it was then. This word is powerful; it is capable even of " saving our souls."

Putting the Word into Practice Properly (1:22–25)

Be Doers of the Word (1:22–24)

[22]*But you must put the word into practice, and not be content merely to listen to it, deceiving yourselves.* [23]*Anyone who is content merely to hear the word and not put it into practice is like a man who contemplates his physical appearance in a mirror;* [24]*once he has studied it and gone away, he immediately forgets what it looked like.*

St. James now uses the catch-phrase everything he has said was leading up to; you must put the word into practice. Practice what you believe. A man may accept the teaching of the faith and recognize it as the truth; he may even go to great lengths to get a truly intellectual grasp of revelation, but if he fails to live a life in conformity with God's will, he is merely fooling himself. Faith such as that is not sufficient for salvation. On the contrary, the knowledge he has will one day prove fatal to such a person, because his life will be judged by what he knew. St. Paul, like

Jesus, had been urgent in insisting on the need for action; those who have learned to recognize God's truth and his will must take their belief seriously. St. James continues Jesus' teaching and sums it up strikingly. This was clearly aimed at saving his readers from a false, self-righteous, and conceited attitude based on the conviction that they were the elect. Yet, his words concern all of us. Nothing could be more mistaken than to imagine that St. James's words refer only to a danger which threatened Jews or Jewish Christians, which has since been overcome. Such an idea is the fruit of the very attitude St. James wishes to uproot. An empty Christianity which is Christian only in name cannot bring a man to salvation.

St. James supports his statement by means of a comparison. A man may study his appearance in a mirror and immediately forget what the mirror told him. In the same way, a man may experience the truth in the light of faith, but continue to live exactly as if the faith had not given him a penetrating insight which should guide his life and behavior. A superficial knowledge of the faith is of no avail.

Salvation is Promised Only to Those Who Do the Word (1:25)

²⁵*If a man has steeped himself in that perfect law which is the law of freedom, and dwells on it, not like one who listens and forgets, but as one who is a doer of the work, he will be blessed in his practice of it.*

St. James here introduces another new image. Living up to our faith means contemplating the doctrine we profess attentively;

above all, it means steeping ourselves in the directives God has given us, adopting them as our own will and living by them. St. James stresses the need for this constant preoccupation with God's will, if we are to practice our faith properly, by calling on us to dwell on it. By his constant preoccupation with God's word interiorly, a Christian must always try to conform to his will, as it is revealed to us. Only then will he be capable of fashioning his whole life in accordance with it.

Is it possible that such a life is merely legalistic piety which has nothing to do with salvation? St. James describes the new law of the Christian life with the wonderful phrase " The perfect law of freedom." The source of this law is God's saving will; its goal is the perfection of redeemed mankind, and it finds its fullest expression in the " royal law " of unselfish love of one's neighbor (2:8; cf. 4:11f.). This law, therefore, springs from the freedom enjoyed by men who have been redeemed from sin, selfishness, and the spirit of the world. It preserves them in this freedom and brings it to its fullest development. It is only as God's child and the firstfruits of his redeemed world that man is truly free to live as his own nature demands he should live.

That is why the promise of salvation is intended for those who are " doers of the work." And it is not merely a question of a salvation to come. This salvation is already at work in the lives of those who have been redeemed and take the new gift of grace which they have received seriously. The salvation which is to come will be nothing more than the visible accomplishment of that saving reality which is already present. This promise comes from Jesus himself. He made it to all those who acknowledge him, not only with their lips, but by keeping his word, by " doing " his will (Mt. 7:21-27). As a result of his " doing " God's will, which according to Jesus' teaching is summed up in the supreme commandment of love, the salvation which is to come is already present in a Christian's life.

The Characteristic Marks of Genuine Devoutness (1:26–27)

Genuine Devoutness not Merely a Matter of Words (1:26)

²⁶*If a person thinks he is devout, but does not control his tongue, so that he is merely deceiving his own heart, his devoutness is vain.*

Another failing Christians are prone to in living their faith is the irresponsible use of speech. In a later passage, St. James returns in greater detail to this dangerous line of conduct (3:1–18). He speaks of it as something which leads to self-deception. We can be sure that he is thinking of the frequently uncharitable and self-righteous judgments, criticisms, censures and condemnations which are common among "devout" people of all times and places, and which are often inspired by envy, jealousy, or vanity (4:11f.). Such faults are frequently cloaked under the guise of disinterested zeal for God's glory and the sanctity of his chosen people. Such service of God—this is the literal meaning of the words translated devoutness and devout—is useless. Such a person serves neither God nor his neighbor; he merely panders to his own self-righteousness, and serves the interests of the prince of this world (3:15). Christ exposed such "devout" zeal as hypocrisy once and for all. It is not pious words or zealous speeches which will help us in God's eyes; it is responsible actions. In this instance, this means taming one's tongue and renouncing all self-righteousness.

Genuine Devoutness Proves Itself in Love of One's Neighbor and in Sanctifying One's Own Life (1:27)

²⁷*This is pure and untarnished devoutness in the eyes of God the Father—visiting orphans and widows in their distress, and keeping oneself unstained by the world.*

Genuine devoutness shows itself in a life of active charity towards one's brothers, and in striving for moral goodness. It is not the observation of various prescriptions concerning ritual purity, or the literal accomplishment of exterior practices of piety, which makes devoutness a form of genuine service of God. Only compassionate, active love for all those who are in distress and need help can do this. The expression " widows, orphans " is a stereotyped phrase to indicate all those who are in need. This must be accompanied by an honest effort to achieve one's own sanctification in the eyes of our Father in heaven, according to the measure of his perfection.

It is the spirit of Jesus and the gospel which speaks in this verse. Our Lord cited purity of heart and active compassion which is ready to help as the sign of true devoutness; this is in contrast to any purely exterior cultual or ritual piety. Our striving after God and his perfection, and our efforts to help our fellow men who are in need, must form a unity, if God is to be pleased with the service we offer him in this world, even in the course of divine service in the strict sense. Neither self-sanctification without love of one's neighbor, nor love of neighbor without self-sanctification, is enough to enable us to stand before God. This is a basic insight which is just as actual today as it ever was; many Christians are tempted to play one off against the other and even, at times, to be proud of this.

AN ATTACK ON PARTIALITY (2:1-13)

St. James now takes up another point which is incompatible with a life lived by faith. This is the preferential treatment given to the rich and the disregard for the poor, which still existed even in Christian churches. This subject is announced in the introductory verse, after which it is dealt with in a lively fashion and illustrated with an example. It is worth noting that the example is formulated by the author himself. However, there can be no doubt that he drew his inspiration from real life.

The Practice of the Faith Must be Kept Free of any Partiality (2:1-7)

Those Who Give Preferential Treatment to the Rich Do Wrong (2:1-4)

¹My brothers, your faith in our Lord Jesus Christ, [the Lord] of glory, must not be accompanied by acceptance of persons. ²Suppose, for example, that a man comes to your meeting, splendidly dressed and wearing gold rings on his fingers, and that a poor man also arrives, clad in an unwashed garment; ³suppose, also, that you look at the man who is well dressed and say, You make yourself comfortable here, while you tell the poor man, You stay there, or sit by my footstool. ⁴Surely, this means that you have made distinctions among yourselves; you have set yourselves up as judges and your attitude is perverse.

Faith in Christ as his Lord who is now exalted in God's glory

frees a Christian from all fearful or calculating adulation of other
" masters," whoever they may be. In our dealings with our
fellow men, we must no longer follow the old false standards of
the world. We must not judge our fellow men by their social
status or the esteem they enjoy, or by their worth in the eyes of
others; we must judge them only by what they are before God.
Before God, however, we are all equal, both as creatures and as
sinners who have now been called to salvation. God sees our
hearts; he does not look at something which is purely exterior.
Standards which are based on a purely worldly viewpoint are
often unjust and contrary to charity. They must not be followed
by Christians in their daily lives, not even in their contacts with
nonChristians. St. James's example is consciously exaggerated
and it refers to people who have no set place assigned to them in
the liturgical assembly. The description he gives later (2 : 6–8;
cf. 5 : 1–6) implies that the rich man in question must have been
a nonChristian who attended a Christian service as a matter of
interest. We can be sure that the poor visitor was in the same
position. The rich man, therefore, was shown to a place of honor
and his hosts were even anxious that he should be as comfortable
as possible, while very little attention was paid to the poor
person. There was no one to show him where he could sit. Consequently, he had to stand, or take a seat on the floor. The preferential treatment given to the rich man, which was obviously
intended to interest him in the Christian community, and the
neglect of the pauper, were equally unChristian. The Christians
responsible were exposed as prejudiced and partial judges; they
were " wicked judges " who betrayed their calling.

Even the Old Testament threatened such " partial " judges
with God's incorruptible sentence. How could such people stand
their ground before him who will judge men by their own stan-

dards, as Jesus tells us (Mt. 7 : 1f.)? How can the Christian faith appear attractive or convincing, if the standards by which Christians live are in complete contradiction to the standards of their faith? There can be no doubt that the lives of many Christians which are in complete harmony with the spirit of the world are a source of great scandal to outsiders. We should ask ourselves, are not such false standards often applied in the lives of Christians and in the church? Are not we ourselves among those who regard this as self-explanatory and normal?

God Has Chosen the Poor to be Heirs of the Kingdom (2 : 5–6a)

5Listen, my beloved brothers! Has not God chosen those who are poor in the world's eyes to be rich in faith and heirs of the kingdom he has promised to those who love him? 6aYou, on the other hand, have dishonored the poor.

Our behavior must be modeled on God's behavior. God in his incomprehensible goodness has excluded no one from his love, not even those who are of little or no account in the eyes of the world. On the contrary, " God has chosen what is of no value in the world's eyes " (1 Cor. 1 : 27). Because of the want they endure, poor people are in a better position than others to appreciate man's need of salvation. Consequently, they are particularly susceptible to God's compassionate love. That is why Jesus loved them especially, and addressed his message of salvation to them, in accordance with God's will. " Blessed are you who are poor; God's kingdom belongs to you " (Lk. 6 : 20). Here, once more, St. James is a faithful witness to his Lord.

This does not mean that those who are rich are excluded from salvation. It means that people must acknowledge God's predilec-

tion for the poor and the socially underprivileged; they must
realize that they are rich in faith, and respect them as such. A
man's real wealth consists in being chosen by God. It is the gift
of faith and the fact that he is an heir to God's kingdom that
make a man truly rich. Those who are chosen are already rich;
those who have faith are already heirs. Consequently, they are
entitled to reverence and love even now. How could anyone
refuse to love those whom God loves? How could anyone refuse
to honor those whom God honors? How could we refuse to be
guided by the norms God lays down? We can see for ourselves
how little this is practiced in our churches. Our fellow Christians
often receive very little honor in our churches, especially those
who seem unassuming, insignificant, or uneducated; they are
not taken seriously. Immediately after leaving the church, we
pass one another by with complete indifference. Often enough,
we have very little love for our brothers whom God has chosen
and loves. " How can a man love God whom he cannot see, if
he has no love for his brother whom he can see?" (1 Jn. 4:20).
Is it not true, then, that St. James's reproach applies equally to
us; " you dishonor the poor."

The Rich Bear the Chief Responsibility for Oppressing Christians (2:6b–7)

**6bIs it not the rich who oppress you; is it not they who drag
you before the courts? 7Are not they the very people who
blaspheme the honored name which has been invoked upon you?**

It is clear that the churches to which St. James writes are made
up of the lowest classes of society. They had endured bitter

experiences at the hands of the wealthy land-owners for whom most of them worked as day laborers (5 : 1–6). Yet it seems this had taught them nothing; they still had a weakness for those who were wealthy and had influence. This gives us an insight into the day-to-day existence of pious Jewish Christians; not only were they exploited, deprived of their rights, and regularly reduced to slavery; they were often insulted because of their Christian faith, and even hauled before the courts. What St. James has in mind is not a real persecution of Christians; yet their Christianity was often the reason why the rich treated those who were dependent on them in a particularly uncharitable, oppressive, and hateful manner. We can be sure that this frequently led to formal charges being laid before the Jewish secular and religious authorities, with the usual consequences.

At the same time, St. James cites the reasons which make it possible for Christians to withstand all this. This is the fact that God and his Messiah, Jesus Christ, have chosen them in virtue of their baptism. At baptism, the name of Jesus is solemnly invoked upon Christians, so that they are Christ's property. They have no reason to be afraid of the rich or powerful any more; they enjoy the love and protection of Jesus Christ, their all-powerful Master. The future is entirely in his hands. St. James's description of what happens at baptism is influenced by the thought of the procedure followed when a person bought a slave. The name of the buyer was invoked upon the person who had become his property and so the purchase was legally complete. In antiquity, a name stood for the person who bore it.

Moreover, in using this formula, St. James consciously adopts a title which had been Israel's glory. The Israelites expressed their consciousness of having been chosen by God as his own people by describing themselves as the people over whom " God's name is named." Through Christ, Christians have become God's true people, his own possession; he chose them in baptism. By standing up for his name, and by their readiness to suffer for it, Christians honor both their Lord and his name. This is what is commanded exclusively, to honor Jesus Christ as the Lord. Consequently, Christians must renounce all false adulation, all hankering after human favor; they may no longer court any human "lords." Christ has freed them from all this and their honor now consists in serving him.

It would be wrong, of course, to condemn all those who are rich. St. James is talking about how Christians should behave; he is not talking about how the rich should behave. What he wants to say here is quite clear, just as what he has to say to us is also clear.

Obey the Royal Law (2:8-13)

The Man who Loves Unselfishly Does Well (2:8)

⁸*However, if you obey the royal law in accordance with the scriptures: Love your neighbor as yourself* (Lev. 19:18), *you do well.*

St. James now describes the proper attitude towards one's fellow men. This is unselfish love of one's neighbor, a love which is like that which a person has for himself, as God has already commanded it in the Old Testament. He calls this commandment the royal law for two reasons. He means, first of all, that the whole revelation of God's will as it is found in "scripture," that is, in the Old Testament, and as Christ brought it to perfection (cf. Mt. 5, 17–19), is summed up in this " law." Secondly, he intends to underline the preëminent and even dominating position and importance of this law over all the other moral precepts and commandments. It is only by fulfilling this law that a man obeys God's will and becomes heir to the promises he has made.

St. James refers here, not to the words of Jesus Christ, but to the Old Testament, because he was writing to Jewish Christians. This is the supreme commandment of Christianity; on it " the whole (Jewish) law and the prophets depend," and it was already imposed in the Old Testament. The precept of love of God is not mentioned, because St. James's argument does not demand it. A Christian is chosen out that he may live a life which is in complete harmony with God's saving will. Christ made known God's will perfectly by the prominence he gave to this royal precept. By so doing, he summed up all the particular commandments, precepts, and laws in one supreme commandment. The people of the New Covenant represent the perfect accomplishment of the old chosen people, because God's will, which is the source of the covenant, has been fully revealed to them in Jesus Christ. As a " royal race " (1 Pet. 2:9), we must make every effort to live a life in keeping with this " royal law."

A Person Who Acts Partially Incurs the Guilt of Sin (2:9–11)

⁹*But if you show partiality in your dealings with people, you commit a sin; the law shows that you are a transgressor.* ¹⁰*Anyone who observes the whole law, but stumbles over one [point], has become guilty before the whole [law].* ¹¹*He who said, You shall not commit adultery, also said, You shall not kill. If you*

are guilty of murder, even though you are not an adulterer, you have transgressed the [whole] law.

Partiality in dealing with one's fellow men makes the amount of respect and love we should show him depend on his social status. Such an attitude is a grave offense against the fundamental precept of unselfish love. In that case, our neighbor is not really regarded as a fellow human being who was created by God in the same love as we ourselves and called to salvation. We do not really look upon him as being endowed with the same excellence or enjoying the same right to respect as ourselves. We esteem him only in the measure in which we can expect some increase of honor, good will, or influence from him. In this way, we demean a person created in God's likeness and try to make use of him for our own ends, and by so doing we sin against God's will. This is not by any means only a question of a human failing, an understandable but harmless imperfection; God's will is an integral whole. Anyone who contravenes it in one matter or in one point offends against the very essence of the divine will which is made known to us in the " law of love " (cf. 4:11–12). All the commandments of the second table of the law are rooted in this one precept. Only the man who loves his neighbor as himself will be able to stand before God's judgment seat. God's will is based on love, and love is its ultimate goal.

This shows us how well St. James had understood Jesus' teaching that all sin springs from lack of love. Sin is vanquished and the world is healed only when pride, self-seeking, and lack of love are banished from men's hearts. Consequently, nothing which offends against reverent, unselfish love can be taken lightly; it must be combated energetically if Christ's royal freedom is to dwell in those who are his own.

Follow the Law of Freedom (2:12–13)

*12Speak and act as men who are to be tried in accordance with
the law of freedom. 13A merciless judgment will be pronounced
on the man who does not show mercy. Mercy [however]
triumphs over judgment.*

The law a Christian is subject to is the law of freedom, the law
of love. Through Christ, God has called him to love and chosen
him as his child and heir. He has made him capable of loving
and delivered him from the evil powers of sin and from the
diabolical tyranny of his own ego. In addition, he has freed him
from all slavery to the letter of Jewish legalism. In all his thinking, deciding, listening, speaking, or acting, a Christian must
be inspired by the freedom he enjoys as a result of his love for
God and his neighbor. A man who has not practiced love cannot
stand before God, no matter how perfect he may have been in
practicing virtue or doing good works. God will judge man
according to the measure of his own free graciousness which is
so generous; that is his freedom. And he will reward man
according to the measure with which man himself judged others;
that is God's justice. Only unselfish and generous love can bring
a man to salvation. God will respond to such love magnificently,
even if the person in question has fallen short of his demands in
many other ways. There is a principle recognized even in the
Old Testament according to which mercy triumphs over judgment. We may ask ourselves what measure awaits us?

Our churches and the communities in which Christians live
would certainly be well off, if everyone lived according to the
" law of freedom," the love which comes from God.

FAITH AND WORKS (2:14–26)

This section is devoted to a problem which forms the whole point of the letter. We can see this even in the extremely lively style; the author illustrates the truth of the principle by casting his thoughts in the form of a lesson or disputation; faith without deeds is dead (2:17–26; cf. 2:14). The sharp contrast drawn between faith and deeds and the choice of Abraham as an example have led some writers to conclude that St. James is reacting against a false interpretation of the teaching of St. Paul about salvation through faith alone (independently of the works prescribed by the Jewish law) (Rom. 3–4; Gal. 3–4).

However, St. Paul himself had already reacted against such misinterpretations (Rom. 6:1–23). This is sufficient to show that the point of the discussion is different in both writers. St. James points out that a faith which does not lead a man to fashion his life in accordance with God's will is unavailing; it cannot bring a man to salvation. St. Paul, on the other hand, was obliged to correct the Jewish belief that a man could be just in God's eyes and merit heaven by relying on his own resources and the perfect observance of all the prescriptions of the law. He had to make it clear that sinful man could not work out his salvation by his own efforts; he must accept it by faith, as a gift from God. At the same time, he also stresses the need for faith to find its expression in love, if it is to be able to withstand the judgment God pronounces. St. James, for his part, teaches that, at the judgment, God will look for the fruits of our faith and reward the faithful accordingly.

Faith Without Deeds is Dead (2:14–19)

Faith Without Deeds is Unavailing (2 :14)

¹⁴*What use is it, my brothers, if a man says he has faith, without having any deeds to show? Can faith save him?*

St. James's question is pointed, but the answer he is aiming at is not that the Christian faith has no power to bring a man to salvation. This is presupposed; the answer he really wants is that " faith without deeds," that is, the orthodoxy of a man's beliefs and convictions, cannot, of itself, enable him to achieve salvation. Of its very nature, faith impels a man to put it into practice, to live by it. A man who does not live according to his convictions, or mold his life in keeping with the new vital powers he has received, does not deserve to be called a believer. Faith is directed towards deeds as surely as the seed is directed towards fruit. A man may have great praise for the values incorporated in Christianity and the blessings it brings; he may willingly acknowledge the profundity of its teachings and its spirit; he may pay tribute to its merits, and its power to promote culture; he may even feel perfectly secure in his faith, but if he does not live it, it is useless. At the judgment, God will examine whether we were obedient, devoted, and loyal; whether we proved our faith by our love. These form the key to eternal life.

It is Only by Deeds That Faith Manifests Itself (2 :15–20)

¹⁵*Suppose a brother or a sister comes along, with no clothes or food for the day,* ¹⁶*and one of you says to them: Go in peace,*

warm yourselves, and eat your fill, without giving them anything for their bodily needs, what is the use of that? [17]*It is the same with faith; if it has no deeds to accompany it, it is dead.*

St. James exposes the senselessness and the futility of such faith by means of a consciously far-fetched example. In the light of such apathy and callousness towards the needs of his fellow Christian and the fundamental law of love, the greeting a Christian gives his brother and his apparently sympathetic words appear as hypocrisy. Indeed, such a faith is dead; it has only an appearance of reality. The Christian in this case knew what he should do; he even pays lip-service to it, but he makes no move to put his convictions into practice, not even in a case of extreme necessity such as this.

St. James's proof is compelling. And yet, how willingly we avoid the most self-evident demands of our faith, especially in the vital domain of fraternal charity! St. James is forced to penetrate into the ·farthest recesses of our selfish, self-righteous, and hypocritical reluctance, in an effort to put it right. No other choice must be left us; we must be forced to take God's demands seriously. That comfortable tepidity, indifference, and half-heartedness which feels itself so safe must never be allowed to dominate our lives.

[18]*Perhaps someone will say, You have faith, but I have deeds! Show me your faith which has no deeds, and I will show you my faith by my deeds.*

In a very abbreviated form, St. James here cites an objection which could be made against his line of thought; what is the use of deeds without faith? It is faith that matters, and I have that! Strictly speaking, this objection is well-founded. In contrast to nonChristians, Christians have received the great gift of salvation on the grounds of their faith. This is the gift of a new life, the pledge and inheritance of God's kingdom, which no human activity could ever attain by its own efforts. This is the foundation of all salvation.

On the other hand, this does not entitle us to overlook the need to let this gift find expression in our daily lives. Therefore, this objection is merely an excuse. Only a person who has faith, that is, who lives according to the convictions of his faith, is capable of performing the deeds demanded by faith. If a person has no such deeds to show, his faith is dead. He has allowed God's gift of salvation to become atrophied; only living faith is real faith.

¹⁹*You believe: " There is [only] one God "* (Deut. 6:4). *You do right; [but] the demons also believe [this] and tremble.* ²⁰*Senseless man, do you really want to see that faith without deeds is of no avail?*

St. James takes up the introductory phrase of the prayer " Listen Israel " which was recited three times a day by the Jews at the time of our Lord. On Mount Sinai, Moses had used this phrase to encourage the chosen people to be loyal to the covenant they had made with God (Deut. 6:4). What is the use of reciting a profession of faith in the one true God, if this faith and the need to do the will of God are not taken seriously? Even the demons know what is involved in such a profession; indeed, in many ways their insight is greater than that of a human being who knows only by faith (cf. Mt. 8:29; Lk. 4:34). Yet, their knowledge cannot save them from the condemnation they have incurred. They are denied the opportunity to live a life in accordance with their faith.

The Christian who believes, on the other hand, has every opportunity to work out his salvation. And yet, in our daily lives, we refuse to acknowledge the fact that the mere profession of the faith, which involves only lip-service to it, or a purely intellectual conviction, is not enough. Indeed, it will only make the judgment we must undergo more severe.

The Testimony of Sacred Scripture (2:21–25)

Abraham was Justified by His Deeds (2:21–24)

[21]*Was not our father Abraham justified by his deeds; he " offered up his son Isaac on the altar of sacrifice "* (Gen. 22:9)? [22]*You see, his faith combined with his deeds, and reached its full development through them,* [23]*and [in this way] the scripture was fulfilled which says: " Abraham believed in God, and this was set down to his credit as justice." He was given the name " God's friend." * [24]*You see: A man is justified because of his deeds and not because of his faith alone.*

In this passage, St. James offers the proof he had already promised (v. 18), that faith shows itself and finds its expression in deeds. For this purpose, he chooses Abraham, the great model of faith and of the faithful. Abraham was the great man of faith, even for the old chosen people; in all his trials, he proved his absolute trust in God. He obeyed his will even when God asked him in his old age to offer up his only heir, on whom the fulfillment of the promise depended. His faith in God had to be proved by his deeds. Not only did he prove himself; it was by this that his faith reached its full perfection and development.

The goal at which such faith is aimed is " justice " or " justification." This is the full possession of life as God's child and the assurance that one is God's heir (cf. 1 : 12.17f.; 2 : 5). The justice which had been promised to Abraham previously (Gen. 15 : 6) attained its full perfection only as the result of the way he coöperated, when his faith was put to the test (Gen. 22 : 9f.). That is why he was given a share in the reward promised to such faith; God made him his " friend." This title of honor illustrated wonderfully the new relationship, an intimate and familiar communion of life, between the Christian who has received the gift of grace and God who condescends to him so graciously.

It is only when his faith proves itself by deeds that a Christian reaches the promised goal—communion of life with God. A " believer " who refuses to fix his eyes on the goal God proposes to him, and cheats himself of the reward of his faith, is foolish. A Christian who feels no joy at the thought of this supreme goal of all our human striving, or does not make every effort to attain it, is poverty-stricken. Like his Master, St. James pleads urgently with Christians who are such only in name, whose Christianity is mere lip-service based on a baptismal certificate, to give proof of their faith.

Rahab was Saved Because of Her Deeds (2 : 25)

²⁵*Was not Rahab, the harlot, also justified because of her deeds? She welcomed those who had been sent, and sent them off by a different way.*

St. James appeals to another example from the sacred writings of the Old Testament which demonstrates even more forcibly the saving power of faith which is expressed in deeds. This is the preservation of the household of Rahab the harlot. She hid the Israelite spies from those sent to catch them and, as a result of her action, was spared from destruction when the city was taken (Josh. 2: 1–15; 6: 17.23). She had heard of the marvels performed by the God the Israelites worshiped, and so she took their part by helping them at a dangerous time. Nowadays we would find this example strange, but St. James here takes up an ancient Christian interpretation which regarded this sinful woman's action as a type or example to be followed by Christians (cf. Heb. 11:31). In the story of Rahab, the early Christians saw an example of God's unfathomable love for sinners, the love which Jesus later revealed so powerfully in his dealings with publicans, harlots, and the outcasts.

However, it was only because of the good deed she performed in a spirit of *faith* that she was saved. This shows us what faith is capable of, even in the case of a sinner; it can save him and sanctify him, if he grasps it enthusiastically and puts it into practice in his deeds, in his everyday life. How is it that we have no faith, or too little faith, in this power which can transform our whole life? We are afraid to let the power of our faith exercise its full influence in our daily lives. Great promises have been made to living, active faith which shows itself in deeds.

Summing Up (2:26)

²⁶*The body without the spirit is dead; in the same way, faith without deeds is dead.*

St. James sums up his discussion of " faith and works " with a simile. The point of comparison in both cases is death. If a body is dead, we must conclude that the life-giving spirit is no longer present; similarly, faith which is not accompanied by deeds forces us to conclude that living faith is lacking. Faith which is not lived, which leaves no mark on a person's behavior, is useless for salvation. It is incapable of bringing a man to salvation; it is dead. Consequently, Christians whose faith is like this are living corpses; they do not really exist in God's eyes. It is no wonder that the Lord, when he returns for judgment, will hurl his condemnation against those whose faith is like that: " Depart from me! I have never acknowledged you " (Mt. 7:23), even though they bear his name and recognize him as their Lord. On the other hand, anyone who listens to the voice of St. James, his faithful servant, will be able to rejoice at his coming and at the thought of being united with him, like Abraham and Rahab. For our part, we should ask ourselves what will the Lord one day say to us?

SINS OF THE TONGUE (3:1-12)

St. James now goes on to deal with another abuse prevalent among Christians to which he has referred so far only in passing (1:19.26), sins of the tongue. First of all, he speaks of one particular occasion of such sins. This was the temptation, common among Jewish Christians especially, to set oneself up in the liturgical assembly as an expert in sacred scripture and a teacher of the faith (3:1). This is followed by a description of the diabolical power latent in an uncontrolled tongue (3:3-12). St. Paul makes use of ideas familiar to Jews and Jewish Christians which paint, in lurid colors, the destructive effects of an undisciplined tongue. However, his appeal that people should control their tongues and bring them into subjection to the spirit of faith and love is binding on Christians of all ages.

Do Not Be Anxious To Be Teachers (3:1-2a)

¹*My brothers, so many of you should not be anxious to be teachers; you know that otherwise we shall be judged more severely.* ²ᵃ*All of us without exception fail in many ways.*

Every adult male Israelite was obliged to make a public speech in the course of the Jewish synagogue service. He had to be able to interpret the scriptures and say a few words aimed at deepening the faith of his hearers by instructing, edifying, exhorting, or comforting them. Jesus himself had done this. There was, moreover, an organized teaching class, doctors of the law and scribes who had studied the scriptures; these enjoyed great prestige. The early Christians continued this practice; among them, too, there was a teaching class which was held in high esteem. Indeed, the principle was laid down that such teachers must be welcomed like our Lord himself; they spoke in his name. It is no wonder that many Christians aspired to be teachers, or that their motives were not always absolutely pure and free from all desire for aggrandizement or honor. St. James himself belonged to this class; he could speak from experience. He knows how to say the right thing, which at the same time reveals his own feelings on the subject. He reminds his readers of the greater responsibility a person has if he speaks in God's name. In all such matters, the faith and the salvation of the community are involved. A purely human approach, or purely human motive, could lead, not only to misunderstanding, but even to disaster. This is a responsibility which cannot be shirked. If it is true even of an ordinary Christian that he will be called to account for every word he has spoken (Mt. 12:34-37), it is far more true of anyone who proclaims God's word in God's name and interprets it authoritatively. The fate with which the leaders and teachers of the Jewish people were threatened is a terrifying example for them, too.

We can form an idea of the gravity of this responsibility when we consider how poor even those Christians are who occupy positions of authority; they are constantly liable to fail. They bear God's word in weak, in incapable, and often not completely pure hands. St. James's warning, however, does not concern only those who have been entrusted with the office of teaching in the church. It also holds good for all those who have anything to say in the church, for all of us; we constantly set ourselves up as critics and judges of our fellow Christians. We delight in acting as their tutors or schoolmasters, but we are very slow to

listen to a word of advice from anyone else. Often enough an unenlightened zeal, which is not even disinterested, gains the upper
hand, a zeal which is concerned more with its own glory than
with the glory of God. Power in religious matters is the most
dangerous of all forms of power; it enjoys the highest authority
and its binding force extends to the depths of a man's heart.
Hypocrisy and self-deception may easily be concealed under the
good end which is intended. The damage done in the church
in the past by incapable, unenlightened, unworthy, and impure
bearers of God's word in the widest sense is appalling. St.
James's grave warning, therefore, is perfectly appropriate.

Anyone Who Does Not Offend in Speech Is Perfect (3:2b–4)

²ᵇ*If a man does not offend in words, he is a perfect man; he is
capable of keeping his whole body under control. ³If we put bits
into horses' mouths, to make them obey us, we have full control
over their whole bodies. ⁴See also how ships, despite their great
size and the fact that they are driven here and there by strong
winds, are turned by a small little rudder the way the helmsman's touch wants it.*

At first sight, this argument is not very clear. There are many
people who are quite capable of controlling their tongues, but are
far from being perfect. At the same time, St. James here touches
upon a vital point. His remarks are relevant, not only for
excitable Orientals who love to talk, but for us all. A man's
words are the real means by which he acts and conducts his life.
It is by his words that a man gets out of himself and contacts his

fellow men; by them, too, that he shares in the events which affect all mankind.

A man's words have frightening power for good or evil. They are not merely noise or hot air; it is by his words that a man acts and expresses himself, whether they are words of love, devotedness, or attachment, or words of lovelessness, betrayal, mockery, hatred, or destruction. God's divine being and will are revealed to us in his word which effects what it proclaims. Human words express the feelings and desires of the one who speaks them; they influence us and invite us to answer. That is why a man's tongue is the most powerful of all his members. Anyone who succeeds in subjecting his tongue to God's law, has subjected his entire being to him. A man's words express the reality which lives in him. St. James gives a popular and impressive illustration of this under the images of a horse and a ship. Man can control a horse, with his powerful body and fiery strength, only by imposing his will to dominate in the right way and making it prevail. Anyone, therefore, who is determined to be perfect must begin " with his mouth "; he must use the God-given gift of speech responsibly, and be master of the unruly desires and impulses of his heart, which can so easily take control of his tongue.

The comparison with a sailing ship at the mercy of a storm-wind emphasizes this truth even more forcefully. Here, too, it is important to begin in the right way, that is, with the rudder. The touch of the helmsman is enough to make the whole vessel obey his will. A man who starts by reforming his speech will be able to bring his entire being into submission to God's will; he will be able to lead a perfect life. The degree of perfection attained by a man who tries to live according to God's will must be measured by his speech, by the control he exercises over his tongue. If a man fails in this domain, not only does he offend against God's will, but he also has a harmful influence among his fellow men in the world and in the church.

The Destructive Power of the Tongue (3:5-8)

A Source of Evil (3:5-6)

⁵*Similarly, the tongue is* [*only*] *a small organ and* [*yet*] *it boasts great power. See what a great forest a tiny flame can set on fire!* ⁶*The tongue, too, is a fire; it is numbered among the members of our bodies as a world of wickedness; it is a stain on the whole body, and it sets the whole cycle of being on fire, while it draws fire itself from hell.*

It is no wonder that such terrible powers should dwell in men's words, and so in their tongues; this is the power which is behind a man's words. It may be God's spirit and God's will, but it may also be Satan's diabolically evil spirit, with all its destructive tendencies. St. James is anxious to encourage Christians to use the gift of speech well. This is why he stresses the baneful consequences of irresponsible language which comes from a wicked heart. It is like a raging fire which destroys everything within reach. Once evil has gained the upper hand over a person's speech and goes out into the world, it devours all before it until there is nothing left but ashes and ruins. God's is not the only word which has power in the world; Satan's word, too, exercises great influence, through the words spoken by men. The point on which evil hinges and around which it turns is man's heart. It is from this inflammatory source, man's heart, the wheel-hub around which everything revolves, that evil originates, and by means of their words gains the upper hand over the human race and its destiny.

St. James here paints a very dark picture of mankind. In his fallen nature, man is exposed to the influence of Satan and hell. He has become the instrument, the mouthpiece, and the herald of Satan, who was a liar and a murderer from the beginning (cf. Jn. 8:42-47). This is a source of great harm and it makes its effects felt both in the ups and downs of an individual's life and in the course of the generations. This is the meaning of the reference to the cycle of being, the wheel of life, from the center point of which the devouring flames reach out over a person's whole life.

St. James draws his teaching from the revelation Jesus made. The image of the wheel of life has the same meaning as our Lord's words about the flood of uncleanness which wells up from a man's evil heart and defiles everything. We could say that it is pumped out and sprayed around by his tongue. " The seat of wickedness " is rooted in the hearts of men who are enslaved to the spirit of this world. It is from man's evil heart that all wickedness comes, " murder, adultery, impurity, stealing, false witness, blasphemy," all his evil thoughts, wishes, and intentions (Mt. 15:19; cf. Mk. 7:15.21ff.). The whole man, therefore, is defiled by his undisciplined speech which comes from his malicious disposition. So he incurs God's sentence of condemnation.

Everyone must surely have noted with alarm the satanic power such speech wields both in society as a whole and in his own life. There can be scarcely anyone who has not experienced the realization of his own responsibility for such destructive activities. Certainly, our fate and that of the world would be assured, if

we were really conscious of our responsibility for our words, and
purified our wicked hearts, the source of all evil, choking off the
fire of destruction at its base.

Untamed Power (3:7–8)

*⁷All kinds of birds, wild animals, reptiles, and fish are tamed
and have been tamed by mankind. ⁸Yet no one can tame the
tongue, a restless source of evil which is full of deadly poison.*

However, this is not easy. Evil strikes its roots into the very
depths of a man's heart. What a contradiction this involves!
Man is capable of subjecting everything to himself; he can force
everything to serve him as he wishes. The only thing he cannot
tame is himself, his words, his tongue, his heart. What a poor
master he is, incapable of mastering himself, although his God-
given vocation is to be lord of the whole world. This is a fine
allusion St. James makes here. By referring to the four types of
living things, he recalls the commission God gave man to dominate the earth (Gen. 1:26; 9:2). Man must be master and lord
even of his tongue, that restless, and deadly poisonous serpent
which is governed by his evil heart (cf. Ps. 139:4). In this way,
he must be equal to the task committed to him as God's image
to be lord of the world. He must fulfill the vocation he has
received to live in the world in accordance with the will of his
Creator. St. James was writing for Christians, for people who
were already redeemed. His pessimistic conclusion, from which
there is no apparent escape, that no one can control an evil
tongue, involves a pressing appeal to them; are you going to let
this be true in your case too? Or are you unwilling to make good
use of your newly-won freedom from evil and the Evil One?

A Christian's Words
Should Be Words of Praise and Blessing (3:9–12)

The Sad Reality (3:9–10a)

⁹*We praise our Lord and Father with our tongues, and we curse our fellow men " who are made in God's image "* (Gen. 1:26f.) *with them.* ¹⁰ᵃ*Praise and cursing come from the same mouth.*

By speaking in the first person plural, St. James lends great weight to the sharp contrast he makes between what should be done and the sad reality. Cursing one's fellow men does not refer only to the Jewish custom of invoking a curse on the godless, the evil-doers, and all their wicked enemies—a practice which Christ superseded with the command to love one's enemies. It also refers in general to the all-too human attitude whereby people speak ill of their fellow men and rejoice at their misfortune. The contradiction is particularly revolting when Christians who say their prayers piously and attend church services regularly treat their fellow men and fellow Christians uncharitably and hatefully, even though they are children of the same Father and were created by him. Our task, on the contrary, is to love all men, even our enemies, and honor them; we are bound to pray for them and repay good for evil. So we will imitate the example of our Father in heaven who is so good that he surrounds even the wicked with his gracious care; and we will obey Christ's command, following the example he gave us. In this passage, therefore, St. James reminds us indirectly of the " royal law " (cf. 2:8.13). How could a man hope to praise God sincerely, if he abuses God's image and wishes him evil? It is impossible for a person to honor God properly, if he dishonors someone created by him. It is impossible for a person to have real love for God, if he hates and detests his fellow men who are children of the same Father.

The Truth Which is Commanded (3:10b–12)

¹⁰ᵇ*That cannot be, my brothers.* ¹¹*Does a spring give out sweet and bitter water from the same opening?* ¹²*My brothers, can a fig-tree produce olives, or a vine figs? No more can a salt spring yield sweet water.*

Such conduct on the part of Christians is unnatural. In the whole of creation, there is no other example of such contradictory behavior. As God's creature, a man is obliged to honor his fellow men. As a Christian, he must even love them as his brothers. Only such an attitude is in keeping with the divinely established order of the redeemed universe. A man whose actions are not in keeping with his nature does not come from God. His exterior " manifestations " reveal his evil interior which is dominated by the devil; they unmask him as a hypocrite and expose him to God's judgment. A man who is called to praise God as his child must honor and love his brother and wish him well. No other course is open to a Christian.

St. James's pointed questions admit no other answer. That is why he breaks off here abruptly; the matter is self-evident. Being a Christian means using our God-given power of speech in keeping with God's spirit and God's will, with a heart which is good and truly converted. It means employing this faculty in God's service by praising him sincerely, and in the service of our fellow men by using it to express our love and good wishes. When a Christian acts like this, he becomes free from the diabolical tyranny of evil speech. He prepares the way for the saving power of God's word in the world. We should ask ourselves, in whose service is our tongue?

A CONDEMNATION OF THE SPIRIT OF THE WORLD, OF JEALOUSY, AND OF QUARRELING (3:13—4:12)

In this section, St. James attacks the causes of such quarreling, uncharitableness, and tension in the various local churches. He does this by stringing together short groups of sentences which are only loosely connected, and forming a train of thought with them. The evil must be exposed in all its different aspects, and an attempt made to uproot it. First of all, he expounds the basic principle of correct behavior; this is gentle love which is devoted to the service of peace. This is the true wisdom which comes from above (3:13–18). Then he reveals the causes of the existing deplorable state of affairs; selfish, self-centered impulses and actions which are inspired by the as yet unconquered spirit of the world which is still a powerful force in many Christians (4:1–6). Finally, he calls for repentance, for humble submission to God's will (4:7–10), and for the rejection of all uncharitable and self-righteous judgments or criticisms (4:11–12). In so doing, he reduces faults which were, to some extent, particularly frequent to their common denominator, and calls upon all Christians to free themselves from the spirit of the world. The commandment of unselfish and constructive love must be taken seriously, both in their own lives and in the community.

True and False Wisdom (3:13–18)

True Wisdom is Manifested by a Good Life (3:13)

[13]*Who among you is wise and understanding? Let him show by*

201

his good life what he has accomplished, in gentleness and wisdom.

Who would not like to be wise? To have a right understanding of all the circumstances of life, and to be able to see the proper, sensible, and wise attitude to be adopted in the conduct of one's life? For Christians, such understanding has as its object the way to salvation and God's saving design. The wise man is he who understands God's will properly and lives by it. It is clear that the effort to understand God's revelation had led to petty jealousies, quarreling, and tension among some Christians. We know from other sources that this was true of other churches at the time also. It is quite possible that such problems arose in connection with the question of the relationship between faith and works (2:14-26). By way of reaction, St. James emphasizes the fact that genuine wisdom is manifested only by a person's life, and indeed by a life which is governed by love for God. Here once more St. James expresses Christ's will and follows his example (cf. Mt. 5:5; 11:29), as he has already done before (1:21). That man is wise who lives a good, humble, gentle life after Christ's example. The possession of God's inheritance is promised only to such persons (Mt. 5:5).

The Source and the Results of False Wisdom (3:14-16)

¹⁴*If, however, you harbor bitter jealousy and a quarrelsome spirit in your hearts, you cannot afford to boast and lie against the truth. ¹⁵That is not the wisdom which comes from above; it is earthly, natural and diabolical. ¹⁶Where there is jealousy and a quarrelsome spirit, there you will have disorder and every kind of evil behavior.*

The rule for the discernment of spirits which is laid down here shows that the deplorable results of the pride certain Christians take in their wisdom come from an evil source, the spirit of Satan. Jealousy, pride, self-satisfaction, quarreling, and underhand dealings are all opposed to God's spirit. This is the meaning of the expression " natural." These are the source of the wicked actions and behavior of Christians in the church and in their own lives. Anything that is opposed to charity is opposed to the truth; anything which springs from the spirit of the fallen world exercises a destructive influence. Therefore, if a man boasts of being wise, while at the same time he criticizes, condemns, and despises others, thereby causing confusion and divisions in the church, he " lies against the truth." He shows himself in God's eyes as a servant of Satan. It is alarming that so many Christians should still fall into this snare and do the devil's work for him.

The Source and the Results of True Wisdom (3:17–18)

¹⁷*The wisdom which comes from above, on the other hand, is known primarily by its purity; it is also peace-loving, considerate, submissive, and full of mercy; it yields good fruit and is free from partiality or hypocrisy.* ¹⁸*The fruit which is holiness is sown in peace by those who work for peace.*

The wisdom which comes from above, from God, is capable of fulfilling God's loving will. Originating from God, it has power to further God's work in the world, the internal and external growth of his church. Such wisdom is not concerned with exalting or justifying itself; it is concerned only with the disinterested accomplishment of God's will in the community of the faithful. It is in serving the faithful that true wisdom yields its desirable harvest. Man is incapable of living wisely of himself or for himself; this ability comes from God alone and is given to be employed in his service. The wisdom a person strives after by his own efforts or for his own benefit is bound to remain imperfect and even unproductive, in God's eyes. It lacks the proper driving force, the proper guidance, and the proper goal. " If any one of you regards himself as a wise man in this world, he must become a fool, to be really wise. This world's wisdom is foolishness in God's eyes " (1 Cor. 3 : 18f.).

St. James now gives seven marks by which true wisdom is recognized, to show its perfection. Above everything else, it is pure and free from hypocrisy. That is, it is not inspired by a desire for power or influence in the church. It is anxious to please God only and it has no ulterior or selfish motives. That is why it is in a position to foster an awakening of God's Spirit in itself and in the community, following the example of Christ who lived by the Spirit. A truly wise man is full of consideration for everyone, including those who are foolish. He adapts himself to the majority and shows mercy, forgiveness, and practical love to all those who need them (cf. 2 : 14–26). Where the common good demands it, true wisdom renounces its rights and the position it holds. It avoids all forms of quarrelsomeness, cliques, or favoritism; it expends itself consciously in promoting unity and peace in the community and in the church.

The man who behaves like this follows Christ's example and obeys his commandment; he made himself everybody's servant, to bring all men to salvation. Such a man can only bring forth good fruits, like his Master. Everything that promotes the peace

and progress of the church is good. Consequently, truly wise
Christians are those who devote themselves actively to the
preservation of peace in the community. They do this by saying
the right word, inspired by a spirit of responsible fraternal
charity, but above all by unselfish, active love.

Such seed produces lasting fruit. " Blessed are the peace-
makers; they will be called children of God " (Mt. 5:9). God the
Father will acknowledge those who practice such wisdom as his
true children, when he comes to pass sentence on the actions of
all men. Surely we have all experienced already the truth that
only unselfish love is capable of lasting results. It must be clear
to everyone that discord exercises a destructive influence. Why
is it that in our churches our behavior is so little in accordance
with the wisdom God gives, with Christ's love?

Friendship with the "World" Means Enmity with God (4:1–6)

The Spirit of the World the Source of All Discord (4:1–3)

¹*From where do the wars and fighting come which exist among
you? Is it not from this; from your [selfish] lusts which wage
war in your bodies?* ²*You covet something, but you have not got
it. You commit murder and you long for something, but cannot
attain it. You fight and wage war, but you cannot get it, because
you do not pray.* ³*You pray, but you do not receive, because your
prayer is evil; you would waste it on your passions.*

St. James now deals with the sources of false wisdom and its harmful effects, and exposes them without mercy. He speaks passionately in terms taken from military life and the conduct of war. Exaggerating a little, we could say that a state of civil war existed in the churches to which he was writing. The quarrels and tensions which were commonplace among them were obviously rooted in the adverse social conditions endured by the majority, and also in the fact that the mass of poor and very poor Christians was opposed by only a few who were rich (cf. 2:1-9; 5:1-6). The efforts of these poor people to achieve security and ownership were perfectly comprehensible, but they followed the wrong road. The result was serious tension, jealousy, and quarreling between Christians, a sure sign that their motives were purely material and selfish. The hearts and minds of many Christians were—and still are—dominated by self-interest; that was what led to a " state of war " in the communities.

Every good gift, both for the individual and for the church, comes from God (1:17). Therefore, a man must direct all his striving towards him, if peace is to reign " in his own heart " and " in the churches." Peace in this world is rooted in God's peace, which is given to those who live according to God's spirit. It is only by being delivered from the domination of selfish and unrestrained lusts and desires that Christians can enjoy such peace. The sanctification of the world, therefore, can come only from within and from above. Anything coming from a different source is " impious and deceitful."

St. James, therefore, does not completely reject the desires of those who want " to get something out of life." On the contrary, he shows how we may get what we want. We must pray confidently to God for his gifts. We must pray for the things which we really need for our life in this world, for the life which God gives here and now to those who trust in him and do his will. The "lusts," "jealousy," and "quarreling" St. James speaks of here spring ultimately from the desire for life, for a full, rich, and secure life which gives a man joy and satisfaction. This striving is put into man's heart by his Creator. Man is marked out for life. The tragedy is that the world, in its state of estrangement from God, does not know and will not admit that only God has the right to dispose of life. The world believes that it can attain life in all its fullness and extort it by its own efforts. And this independently of God, or even in opposition to him, often enough. This is the law followed by the men of "this world" ever since the original revolt of their father Adam; he was determined to become "like God" by his own efforts (Gen. 3:5).

Such efforts are doomed to failure. They lead to jealousy, hatred, quarreling, and so to death. This is the clear implication of the words chosen by St. James in this connection; jealousy, fighting, war, murder. Murder in the strict sense can be certainly excluded. St. James uses the strong expression "murder" to remind his readers of Jesus' words: The man who hates his brother is a murderer. He envies and begrudges his brother the life which God gave him, just as he gave it to himself (cf. Mt. 5:21f.; 1 Jn. 3:15). How could such pernicious efforts, such destructive behavior lead to life?

Yet Christians pray every day for the saving gift of life; they pray daily for God's blessing. How is it, then, that their unhappy position remains unchanged? Everything is in God's hands; it would cost him nothing to answer the prayers of his faithful in overflowing measure. Jesus, who is the Lord, said: "Ask and you shall receive" (Mt. 7:7) and: "Everyone who asks will receive" (Mt. 7:8). St. James wards off this implied reproach against God by taking up Jesus' words: "You pray (certainly), but you do not receive, because your prayer is evil; you would waste it on your passions " (4:3).

God stands by the promise made by Jesus Christ whom he sent. But the Christians in this case were not praying in the spirit Jesus prescribed, as it is revealed in the Our Father: " Thy will be done." On the contrary, they hoped by means of their prayers to accomplish their own selfish wills and their purely worldly desires. Ultimately, it is the hordes of evil spirits who exercise the mastery over these Christians who are still subject to the spirit of the world. They want to use God's goodness for their own evil ends. It is no wonder that God cannot listen to such prayer. Prayer like that is not aimed at the progress of the life which comes from his hands; it does nothing to promote the growth of his kingdom in this world.

St. James here draws attention to a serious danger which is common to all Christians. This is the primordial temptation felt by all human beings, and especially by those who are devout, to try to subject God to themselves and use him for their own ends. If a man is determined to do this and is constantly at loggerheads with God because he refuses to hear his selfish prayer, it means that he has not taken his Christian faith seriously. Faith means abandoning oneself entirely and without reservation to God's will; it means having a childlike trust, and saying in all circumstances: " May your will, not mine, be done " (Mk. 14:36). It is precisely by a Christian's prayer that we know whether he is still subject to the spirit of the world, or whether he has real faith. It is this which shows us whether he is prepared to leave everything in God's hands, and receive from him everything which it is God's will to give him in his love and saving power. It is worthwhile frequently examining the sincerity of our own faith in the light of this standard.

God Wants Our Whole Selves (4:4–6)

⁴[You] adulterers! Do you not know that friendship with the world means enmity with God? That, consequently, anyone who is determined to be a friend of the world, proves himself God's enemy.

For a Christian, surrender to the spirit of this world, to the spirit of the prince of this world and his henchmen, means turning away from God. It means coming to terms with God's enemy, which is a form of adultery. St. James here takes up the image of a bond of marriage and love which the prophets used to describe the relationship between Israel and its God. Like St. Paul, he applies it to the relationship between God and the church, the new people of God. The church is God's bride; the Messiah won it as his own by his death. " I have betrothed you to one man, to present you to Christ as his spotless bride " (2 Cor. 11:2).

St. James takes up this idea by addressing his readers as " adulterers." Every baptized Christian who has been called by God stands in an indissoluble union of life and love with God. Anyone who does not respond to God's love with his whole heart, but keeps an eye out for other " lovers," violates this loving union. Such a person wants another friend, the fallen world, which is here regarded as being God's enemy. In so doing, he shows that he really loves only himself in the last analysis. We should take these words to heart. They serve to remind us again and again of the betrayal involved in every form of half-heartedness, in all " leaning towards both sides," in all toying or dallying with the spirit of the world. In this appeal for wakefulness, which is really a threat of judgment, we can hear Christ's bitter complaint: " I have this against you; you have abandoned your first love " (Rev. 2:4).

Therefore, anyone who prefers to side with the spirit and the children of this world in his life, rather than with God, " proves himself " God's enemy and a traitor to him. Between the " world," which is dominated by the spirit of God's enemy, and God, no compromise is possible. The man who is not subject to God and united with him in a spirit of obedience is an " adulterer "; he is a traitor to God's love. God does not look only for some crumb of our love. He does not want merely a series of acts of obedience to the law which are outwardly unobjectionable. He is not interested in emotional hours of fervor inspired by the celebration of Sundays or feastdays. God wants our hearts; he wants our whole selves. " You shall love the Lord your God with your whole heart, with your whole soul, and with all your strength."

⁵Or do you think scripture means nothing, when it says: " He longs jealously for the spirit he has made dwell in us "?

What does St. James mean with this quotation about God's " jealousy "? The good spirit God has sent to man, the " new I " with which Christians are endowed, must not be supplanted by the spirit of this world which is evil, that is, by worldly passions. A Christian in this world, therefore, is at war and the struggle takes place in his own heart. The " new I " with which a person is endowed who has been born anew by faith and baptism must assert itself. It must overcome the evil impulses which have their origin in a person's " members," that is, in the

fallen ego of the man in whom redemption has not reached its
full perfection.

In such circumstances, it is a help to know that God keeps
watch over his good spirit. The realization that God will one day
demand that we should return the good spirit he has given us
is an inducement to do our utmost. Indeed, he already claims
this spirit for his service even here and now, as an answer to
his love. God demands man's love exclusively for himself and
for his will. This demand is based on his own total love by
which he has called men to share his love in deepest intimacy.
God watches " jealously " over the covenant of love he has made
with every baptized Christian. He will demand an account from
everyone who sins against this union of love, whether treacher-
ously or frivolously. God has given us the gift of a new being
which means that we now possess real life for the first time.
What other return can we make for such love, except by loving
him exclusively? It is impossible for real love not to be jealous
of the love of the one who is the object of such love. Surely we
should be grateful that God's love watches over us so jealously,
for our salvation.

⁶*But he gives a grace which is all the greater, so that we are
told: " God opposes the proud, and gives grace to the humble
man "* (Prov. 3:34).

God loves those who are his own and promotes their salvation.
This is what St. James wants to prove by his quotation from
scripture. Even God's jealousy and his action in correcting us are
in the service of his redeeming love. When he intervenes to
correct or punish us, when he demands our whole selves, this is

to prepare those whom he loves to receive an even greater share of his favor and grace, an even greater share of God's love. If a person wants to receive a present, he must open his hand. If a person want to receive God's love in a becoming manner, he must free his heart from all self-glorification and from attachment to the world. The spirit of the world reaches a climax in the self-exaltation and overbearing pride which sets itself up as God and regards itself as the center of all. That is why God opposes the proud with their evil hearts, and gives his grace only to those who are humble and open to receive it. Like Mary, such people realize that everything good, everything exalted, everything with any real value comes from God.

This is a basic principle of the redemption, and it was recognized and expressed even in the Old Testament, as the quotation shows. For us, however, it is of fundamental importance. When God sent his Son, he was born of a humble virgin on whose lowliness God had looked graciously, while he rejected all that is exalted and overbearing in this world (cf. Lk. 1:47ff.). As God's Suffering Servant, his Son dispossessed himself of his majesty and underwent the final humiliation in the shame of the cross. This was the attitude he demanded of his servants: " Learn from me, for I am meek and humble of heart " (Mt. 11:29). God gives himself wholly to anyone who opens his heart without reservation to his love, and surrenders to his will. But that is not easy. Our self-centered fallen nature forces its way into the center of our hearts and tries to make God's love serve its own ends. We need to renounce all self-seeking and self-glorification again and again, and open our hearts to God. It is only the determined rejection of the spirit of the world, accompanied by a return to God, which can make us capable of union with God.

Take Your Faith Seriously (4:7–12)

Therefore, You Must Be Converted and Return to God (4:7–10)

⁷Submit to God, therefore! Stand firm against the devil and he will flee from you.

Finally, St. James calls upon his readers to renounce all half-heartedness and submit completely to God's will. Faith means obeying God, submitting one's own will to God's, recognizing God as the Lord and ruler of one's life. " Your will, not mine." Submission to God alone shows whether a person's faith is sincere. It is only such submission that makes a person who has already received a call from God a believer. He leaves the world and its sphere of influence, overthrows the throne of his self-glorifying fallen nature, and enters God's domain. The man who does God's will loves God. Neither the devout profession of the faith nor the exterior practices of piety, of themselves, can achieve this. With this uncompromising demand, St. James once more bears witness to the teaching of our Lord Jesus Christ (cf. Mt. 7:21).

The Yes we say to God must be borne out by the No we say to the devil. Between God and Satan no compromise is possible. The constant struggle against the temptations and threats of the devil is essential to Christianity. No one can avoid it, because no one can serve two masters (Mt. 6:24). We must serve God or Satan.

We must remember, too, that the man who has decided for God, completely and without reservation, is not alone. God stands by him and clothes him with the armor of his invincible might. "If God is for us, then who can be against us?" (Rom. 8:31). Not only can such a person not be overcome; as his own experience will soon teach him, Satan flees before him. In the presence of God's power, he is forced to recognize the failure of all his wiles and acknowledge his own powerlessness.

⁸Draw near to God, then he will draw near to you. Purify your hands, you who are sinners; sanctify your hearts, you who are in two minds. ⁹Lament, mourn, and weep. Let your laughter be turned to mourning and your joy to sadness.

Here, too, Christians must beware of a false security. Turning to God is not merely a matter of an intellectual decision. It must find expression in prayer; it has need of prayer, in which it is constantly renewed. It is by prayer that we gain access to God's love, in prayer that our surrender to him finds expression in trust, entreaty, obedience, gratitude, and praise. God, for his part, listens to every prayer which comes from a sincere heart. In this way, he draws near to a Christian, and the Christian becomes ever more deeply involved in a union of love with God. Full of grateful joy, he experiences the wealth of God's graciousness. Such prayer, however, must come from a pure heart. Only the pure and sinless can draw near to God who is so holy. That is why the renunciation of all halfheartedness and all worldly attitudes is so necessary. The indecision which makes it impossible to choose once and for all between God and the world, which comes from lack of faith, must be replaced by a firm decision to choose God. The power Satan enjoys springs from the weakness of Christians who are in two minds, whose faith and prayer are halfhearted. God's remoteness is caused by man's indecision and lack of faith; it is not the result of God's superiority to the world or of his self-sufficiency. This is an important point to remember for anyone who is determined to take his faith seriously.

There can be only one conclusion; a Christian must acknowledge his own wretched condition and deplore it sincerely. A melancholy frame of mind which is sceptical is of no avail. This is the meaning of the repeated and ever more intense appeals for practical sorrow and conversion. How much misery is often concealed behind a mask of worldly contentment and busy happiness. Often enough, an unworthy compromise is reached in this way with a person's own wretchedness, from which in all honesty he has no desire to escape. This will not do; a Christian must acknowledge his wretchedness; he must detest and confess it, if he is to escape from the state of slavery to himself and Satan's tyranny, and come close to God. The coming of God's kingdom presupposes conversion and penance as its necessary prerequisite (Mk. 1:14f.). Those who shy away from this will always be in two minds; they can never draw near to God.

¹⁰*Humble yourselves before the Lord, then he will exalt you.*

" Humility " is also necessary (cf. 4:6). A person must empty himself and renounce all attachments to his own selfish lower nature and the spirit of this world. He must acknowledge his sinfulness, his misery, and his helplessness. Anyone who submits obediently to God's will, will experience in his own life the basic law of the redemption: The man who seeks himself will lose himself; the man who gives himself to God will find himself (Jn. 12:25). This is what Jesus told us: " The man who exalts himself will be humbled, but the man who humbles himself will be exalted " (Lk. 14:11).

However, if a person is to be able to appreciate this reversal of values, he must judge by God's own standards. Only a person who has faith will experience this exaltation; only he will be capable of " seeing " it. Such a person judges with God's eyes; he sees himself, his life, and the whole world in the light of God. At the same time, he realizes that we will not be definitively exalted until Christ's second coming. Now that Jesus has died, risen, and been glorified, this final order of things is near, pressingly near. This final state of things already makes its influence felt in the present; it determines and marks the present which, in turn, is pressing on relentlessly towards the final completion of all things. " The Judge is already at the door " (5:9). That is why no one can afford to be slow about repenting. Now is the time to make a serious effort to turn to God. God's claim, God's invitation, as well as our own misery allow no postponement. God's love must not be abused or betrayed. It is in his love that God is determined to exalt us.

Above All, Do Not Judge (4:11–12)

¹¹Do not calumniate one another, my brothers. The man who calumniates his brother or judges him, calumniates and judges the law. And if you set yourself up to judge the law, you do not fulfill the law, you censor it. ¹²There is [only] one Lawgiver, one Judge, he who has the power to save and to destroy. And you, who are you to judge your neighbor?

St. James now comes to the cardinal point of this section, the mutual gossiping and disputing his readers indulged in. They were guilty of disparaging and lowering one another's char-

acter, a fault which can at times lead to calumny. It is true
that all this can be camouflaged under the mask of pious zeal for
the spiritual perfection of one's brother and the community as a
whole. Ultimately, however, it springs from an uncharitable
and self-righteous heart, and it destroys all community spirit.
St. James obviously had good reason to be anxious. The practice
of biting and uninterrupted mutual criticism was becoming a
serious threat to the various local churches. He exerts himself
again and again to eliminate this danger (1 : 19–21.26f.;
3 : 1–4.12; 5 : 9). That is why he chooses such strong words to
describe this continual gossiping, censoriousness, criticism, and
fault-finding; he is anxious to expose the attitude they conceal—
calumniating and judging. The man who behaves like this does
not act in the service of God's holiness and justice. On the contrary, he violates the " royal law," the " law of freedom," which
calls for unselfish, reverent love of one's neighbor. This divine
commandment is the center of all the commandments. It includes all the " commandments of the second table " of the law,
as God gave it to Moses (cf. 2 : 8–13).

The man who regards his brother in a spirit of lovelessness
and speaks self-righteously against him, acts contrary to God's
will; he violates God's " basic law " (Lev. 19 : 15–18). Indeed,
he even sets himself up against God's law as a new lawgiver.
He no longer takes the standard laid down by God as the norm
by which he guides his judgments and his actions; instead, he
takes his own self-righteousness as his norm. Such pharisaical
self-exaltation is contrary to the fundamental obligation in-
cumbent on all God's creatures, to " do " the will of the " Lord
God." At one and the same time, it is a presumptuous denial
of God's sovereignty and of his supreme power to determine
the way of salvation and perfection in complete freedom. The

life and death, the salvation or condemnation of all men, are in God's hands alone.

Anyone who criticizes God's commandments and God's way of salvation, and wants to better the human race according to his own ideas, is a rebel against God. There are some who think they can forge a " pure church " on God's behalf, a church made up of the perfect and just, by pitiless criticism, apparently inflexible realism, and merciless extremism. They act contrary to God's will and contrary to the will of his humble Spokesman who gave his life for sinners. Everyone who judges others or condemns them self-righteously, judges and condemns himself, in the last analysis. Who is just in the eyes of God who is all holy? When God proclaims his judgment, every human being must acknowledge that he is a sinner. And the law by which God judges is the basic law of love. Who can say, with a clear conscience, that he has fulfilled the fundamental law of love of one's neighbor perfectly, that he is really a " doer of the law "? In the light of this divine standard, the words we so often speak about the lack of love, egoism, and hard-hearted self-satisfaction of our fellow Christians and our fellow men are exposed as hypocrisy. It would be much better for us all and for the church if, when we are tempted to judge or condemn others rashly, we asked ourselves the question: " And you, who are you to judge your neighbor?"

A CONDEMNATION OF PRESUMPTUOUS
SELF-ASSURANCE (4:13—5:6)

This section is written in the style adopted by the prophets of the Old Testament when they threatened the people with the divine judgment. It condemns two typical examples of the worldly outlook and behavior which were castigated so severely in the previous section (cf. 3:15; 4:1–4), the presumptuous self-assurance of business people (4:13–17) who are solely intent on the things of this world, and the smug, selfish hard-heartedness of the self-satisfied rich (5:1–6). Both these sub-sections begin with the same invitation: "Come, now," "Now, then." This is an appeal to those whom St. James addresses to submit to God and listen to the sovereign claim he has on them. He will appear soon, and he will quickly convince them how foolish their attitude is. A lively consciousness of the immediate proximity of the divine judgment (and the second coming of Christ) forms the background of this threatening prophecy. This imminent expectation of the last judgment was not realized directly, yet the gravity of this appeal and the demand it makes are justified for all time. No one who is determined to take his Christian faith seriously, no one even who lives and works in this world, can afford to turn a deaf ear to this appeal, if he is not to be exposed as a fool in God's eyes.

Woe to the Self-Assured (4:13–17)

God Alone Disposes of the Future (4:13–14)

¹³*Come now, you who say: Today or tomorrow we shall travel to such and such a town, spend a year there, do business, and*

make a profit. ¹⁴*You say this, you who have no idea what to-morrow will bring. [Indeed,] what is your life? You are only a wisp of smoke which appears for a short while and then vanishes.*

The examples St. James quotes here of people who have allowed themselves to become completely preoccupied with the things of this world in their self-assurance are typical. They are not meant to refer to any particular persons in the various local churches whom he wished to bring to repentance. On the contrary, St. James uses the example of these highly-esteemed and influential persons to show the stupidity of the presumptuous spirit of the world. The man who fails to take God or the brevity of his own life into account, and makes his plans independently of God, is a fool if, despite all this, he still thinks his position in the world is assured. He omits from his calculations the most obvious of all human experiences—man's powerlessness to determine the future. It is not only that man cannot determine the future; he does not even know what it may bring. Tomorrow is an unknown quantity. This is self-evident, so much so that the façade of certainty such busy planners make a display of fails to conceal not only their arrogance, but also their stupidity and blindness. If this is so, what is man of himself, if not a wisp of vapor devoid of substance, which quickly disappears leaving no trace. St. James affirms the emptiness, not only of life in general, but of man himself, of men who share this outlook: " Indeed, you are only a wisp of smoke!"

This is something which must be obvious to everyone. Every worldly advantage involving rank or title, power or riches, influence or importance, must be judged in the light of this. This norm frees a man from envy, greed, bitterness, and from difficulties concerning the faith; it enables him to appreciate things at their true and only lasting value. It is by this that we must judge our own plans and our own aims, our own outlook on life. If we do this, we will have no trouble in arriving at the conclusion: All our certainty must come from God alone. The man who fails to take God into account at every turn is a fool, a nonentity which will quickly vanish.

Presumptuous Self-Assurance is Sinful (4:15-17)

15Instead of this, you should say: If the Lord wills it, we shall live and do this or that. 16As it is, however, you take pride in your boastfulness. All such boasting is evil. 17If a man, therefore, knows how to do what is right, but does not do it, it is sinful in him.

There is no need, however, to let things go, simply because everything is meaningless and uncertain in itself. On the contrary, we must place our trust in God, and submit to his providence and his will in all things. Humble submission to the will of the all-knowing Creator and Lord will save us from placing our confidence foolishly in ourselves. It will also free us from the feverish activism which is inspired by the belief that we can work out our own happiness. When we submit to God in this way, we become aware that we are taken up into a plan of salvation devised by our Father who watches over everything great or small, exalted or lowly, in a wonderful way (cf. Mt. 6:25-34). We realize, too, that the difficulties we meet, and even our heavy crosses, must inevitably turn out for the best (Rom. 8:28). In this way, our prayer " If God wills " gradually becomes " As God wills." Instead of pursuing our own aims, we finally accept God's providence. Only God is capable of giving us life in all its fullness, that life for which man hopes and strives in the future. He will give it to those who trust his leadership.

How is it, then, that so many human beings refuse God's love, although they are indebted to him for everything? They are determined to gain control of the future and win life for themselves by their own efforts and their own resources. How is it that we so easily attribute any good in our lives to ourselves? That we take pride in our own ability, our own strength, our own discretion, our own enlightened foresight, our own success? Anyone would think we had only ourselves to thank for all this. Why is it that so many hold religion as merely a means of escape from the difficulties of life, another way of compensating for one's own failure and weakness, a sign of interior anxiety and cowardice? " What have you that you have not received? And if you have received it, what are you boasting about, as if you had not received it?" (1 Cor. 4 : 7).

There can be no doubt that such pride in oneself is nothing less than boastful presumption, in the last analysis. Consequently, it is sinful. It detracts from God's honor by refusing to show him the gratitude which is his due. It installs a person's own ego in the place of God and offers it a reverence and self-adulation which is idolatrous. The faith professed by the people St. James attacks is centered on " My wish," " My deserts," " My honor," not " Your grace," " Your will," " Your honour." It is no wonder that such an attitude draws down God's sentence upon it.

Not only is such presumption foolish; it is also dangerous. It exposes those guilty of it to God's judgment. St. James lays down the general conclusion in a saying which is almost proverbial in character: Anyone who acts against his better judgment and his conscience is guilty of sin. This is intended to forestall any misinterpretation which would limit the force of his words to those who are outside the church and belong to the world. That is not what St. James means. Christians, too, are constantly exposed to the danger of adopting a self-assured and even presumptuous line of action. The subtlest form of such boastfulness and pride is spiritual conceitedness, a vice which St. James attacks in a number of passages in his letter (1:9ff.; 1:26; 2:1ff.; 3:1f.9–18; 4:11f.). This passage shows us once more how anxious he was to close the gap between faith and practice, and make a Christian's profession of faith bear fruit in a life of faith. It is only by living up to what we believe, by doing God's will, that we can attain salvation.

Woe to the Rich with Their Hard-Heartedness (5:1–6)

Sentence is Already Being Passed (5:1–3)

¹*Come, now, you who are rich. Weep and bewail the misery which is coming upon you.* ²*Your riches are decaying; your clothes have become food for moths.* ³*Your gold and silver are covered with rust, a rust which will bear witness against you and consume your flesh like fire. You have amassed treasures in an age which is the last period of time.*

In virtue of his prophetic authority, St. James in this passage extends the woes Jesus himself pronounced on those who are rich and well fed, on the gluttonous and the voluptuous (Lk. 6:20f.). Now that Christ has risen from the dead and entered into glory, the last stage of time has begun; sentence has already

been passed on the world. Victory and the power which goes
with it already belong to him who has taken his place at the
Father's right hand as the Lord who enjoys full dominion. The
great reversal of values is already underway. All the good things
of this mortal world, together with all those who cling to them
and abandon themselves, have already been taken up into this
process of devaluation and revaluation which will turn everything upside down. Judgment has already been pronounced on
them, and on all those who have no other claim to wealth than
these mortal possessions. This is the situation in which St. James
addresses those who are " rich "; he leaves them in no doubt
about their powerlessness, their lack of security, and their poverty.
His appeal to them to mourn is an anticipation of the lament
they will raise at the sentence which inevitably awaits them.

The misery to which those whose wealth is confined to the
things of this world must look forward is terrifying. The wealth
on which they rely, the source of the worth, the esteem, the
influence, and the pleasure they enjoy, proves deceptive. And
this was the very thing to which they looked for security. It
could not withstand the inroads made by the passage of time.
The rust and the moths will bear witness against these wealthy
people and pitilessly expose their hard-heartedness. They preferred to see their wealth decaying, and made no effort to help
those who were in need with it. Their own hard-heartedness
will be their downfall.

Here, too, St. James leaves the rich in no doubt, not only of
their guilt, but also of their senselessness. Christ's life and the
fate he suffered should—and, indeed, must—have made it clear
to them that his coming marked the beginning of the last stage
of time. Yet they behaved as if the world were going to remain
in its present state for ever, as if God were not soon to reveal

himself in the world as its Judge who will fashion it anew. Now that Christ has come, been put to death, and risen again, Christians are bound to fix their eyes on the end of the world. Those who refuse to do this, and make the good things of this world the goal of all their selfish, cold-blooded striving, are to be numbered among these poverty-stricken rich. Those who are satisfied with such possessions and secure in their self-assurance are fools for whom we can only weep. This is true, not only of St. James's day, but also of our own; not only of those outside the church, but also of those who are in it. God's sentence has already fallen upon them.

Injustice Calls Out to God for Vengeance (5:4-6)

⁴See how the wages of the laborers who reaped your fields, which you have held back, cry out, and the appeals of the reapers have reached the ears of the Lord of Hosts. ⁵You feasted on earth and indulged yourself; you have fattened your hearts for " the day of slaughter." ⁶You condemned the Just Man; you murdered him, he offers no resistance.

St. James is thinking particularly of wealthy landowners. These, of course, were not members of the church, but we can be sure there were Christians among the laborers they employed. They exploited these brutally and even refused them the minimum wage guaranteed by the law of Moses, which had to be paid in the evening. The laborer who did not get this was condemned to go hungry, together with his family. In addition, these wealthy landlords employed their power against the poor in their struggle to vindicate their rights. They defrauded them and deprived them of their rights. They even went so far as to condemn them unjustly and have them put to death. We can be sure that these employers were influenced by the faith of their Christian workers which they hated, as was implied in an earlier passage (2 : 6f.). This was quite possible, because of the partiality and corruption which were common among judges at the time. However, the reference is primarily to the social and economic ruin inflicted on the underprivileged classes. In the book of Jesus Sirach, the exploitation of workers is regarded in the same light as murder (Sir. 34 : 22).

The wealthy classes St. James had in mind, therefore, were unscrupulously selfish. They were interested not in what was right or just, but in increasing their wealth and enjoying life to the full. The hardships the poor endured and the sufferings of their own laborers had no effect whatever on them. On the contrary, this made it easier for them to increase their wealth at any price, by exploiting their workers, by defrauding them of their wages, by oppressing them, and by abusing their rights even to the point of murder. All they were interested in was feasting and reveling. It is no wonder that their hearts had become completely hardened, dulled, enslaved to the world, and "fattened." Their own hungry belly was really their god (cf. Phil. 3 : 19). They failed to recognize the gravity of the situation; now that Jesus has been raised to glory, the last stage of time, the time of judgment, the " day of slaughter " has begun. God's judgment has been handed down; all that remains now is for it to be proclaimed publicly. That is why St. James can speak as he does; the behavior of the " rich " has already been subject to God's scrutiny and judged. There can be no doubt God takes the part of the oppressed. This is especially true if they entrust their well-being completely to him and live like " just men."

St. James is not speaking only for the Christians who found themselves in the situation he describes. Far from it. God takes the part of the poor, the exploited, the oppressed, and the unjustly persecuted in every situation, if they trust him and bring their complaints to him. It is important to realize this. Those who are given to the pleasures of the world and enjoy its power may be quite unscrupulous in their presumption; they may live as they please, with apparent impunity, but in God's eyes they are fools, and sentence has already been passed on them. Now that Christ has been raised to glory, God's judgment has already been pronounced in principle. This does not mean that we can afford to be passive spectators; we have an obligation to work for social justice. Yet, our real hope is in God.

AN APPEAL FOR PATIENCE AND PERSEVERANCE (5:7-11)

In this section, St. James gives us a résumé of the plea he makes in his letter and relates it explicitly to the end of the world which is near. In the sufferings they endure from their fellow Christians who are still imperfect and from the pagans among whom they live, it is important for Christians to keep their eyes fixed on the end of all things. The Lord who is coming will judge justly and punish those who deserve it, but he will also reward in overflowing measure those who have an active faith which has proved itself by perfect fidelity. That is why Christians must be careful not to lose heart; they must keep their eyes fixed on the Lord, who is already at the door, and trust in his goodness. It is this which will bring his elect to a good end, and grant them entrance into God's kingdom in its final form.

Wait Patiently for the Lord's Coming (5:7-9)

Take Heart, the Lord is Near (5:7-8)

⁷Wait patiently, therefore, brothers, until the Lord's coming. See how the farmer waits patiently for the earth's precious harvest; he waits patiently for it, until it receives the early and late rains. ⁸So must you, too, wait patiently and take heart, because the Lord's coming is close at hand.

St. James's letter is inspired by anxiety to arm all the " brothers " for the Lord's coming. Then they will reap the priceless fruit of their faith. Being a Christian means spending one's life preparing for the Lord's coming. It is true that no one knows when he is coming, but it is also true that he is coming, that he is already on the way. That is why the state in which the Lord finds those who are his own will be decisive; his coming will be revealed suddenly and without warning. Only those who are ready will receive the reward, eternal life in God's kingdom. A Christian must be like a farmer and wait for the harvest which will spring from God's word which has been sown in him (cf. 1:17.21). It is then that the Lord will reveal what each Christian has achieved in his life; God's sowing will bear its fruit. The only thing is that Christians must wait patiently and live by his strength; they must live for the Lord's coming. Each year the farmers of Palestine wait confidently with renewed hope for the early rains in autumn, after the crop has been sown, and for the late rains in spring, so that their sowing will not remain fruitless in the hard earth. In the same way, we too must have confidence and trust that God will grant the victory to those who have faith in all the trials the world inflicts on them. Such faith bears fruit which is unique and beyond price, a share in Christ's final and complete victory in God's kingdom.

That is why it is so important to take active steps to overcome all laziness and indifference, all discouragement and want of faith; we must combat the temptation to live by our worldly impulses, and direct our whole lives towards the Lord's coming, happy in the knowledge that those who have faith must inevitably win the victory. And victory is in sight. The Lord's coming is close at hand. St. James here adopts a theme from Jesus' preaching: " The time is up and God's kingdom is close at hand. Be converted and believe the gospel " (Mk. 1:15). Jesus' own life marked the beginning, and ever since then the seed he planted presses on constantly towards the final completion of all things. The Lord is ready now to bring everything into subjection to God's power, and to give those whose faith has been proved by testing a share in his dominion. Ever since Jesus was raised to glory, the whole course of the ages is directed towards the day when God's rule will be complete. Nothing can delay this victory; nothing can change the course on which history is now set. The result has already been decided on Christ's cross. Like the farmer, a Christian may feel that it is a long time to wait; the many dangers to which it is exposed may threaten his hope with extinction; his faith in the final restoration of all things may flag, yet the fact remains that the Lord's coming is near. This is something worth hoping for; this is something which makes it worth our while to take heart in the faith. Only those who have persevered steadfastly will reap the reward.

If our faith has such a small effect on our lives, if our strength is so weak, it is often because we have not a sufficiently vivid conviction that the Lord will come again and that he is near. " Fix your eyes on the goal; wait patiently, and bolster your hearts in the firm conviction that this is the last stage of time." This is St. James's message. If our faith is to bear fruit, it must be fixed deliberately and with stubborn tenacity on the end of all things, on the Lord who is coming.

Do Not Grumble Against One Another; the Judge is at the Door (5:9)

⁹*Do not grumble against one another, brothers, so that you may not be judged. See, the Judge is [already] at the door.*

Often enough, the big problem which confronts our faith is

the life Christians themselves lead in their own communities, not the difficulties of living in a world estranged from God. The lives of Christians in their own communities are often a source of tensions and even scandals of a social, ethical, and religious nature. All Christians are called to practice perfect love, but we are all influenced by the spirit of the world, to a greater or a lesser extent. St. James has no qualms about calling these tensions by their correct name. He, too, was acquainted with the truth which is so often held up to us as a reproach today—Christians themselves are frequently the greatest obstacle to faith in the message of Christianity, the contradiction between what they profess and what they do is so frighteningly obvious. We must all be aware, surely, that such problems have their roots ultimately in our lack of perfect love for our brothers and our fellow men. Genuine love shows itself by its refusal to grumble or find fault. Indeed, it is utterly unselfish and takes the part of those Christians who are a burden to others and least deserving of love. It bears its burden patiently. If a man loves only those who deserve his love and do not offend him in any way, he obviously does nothing extraordinary (cf. Mt. 5:46–48). If a man has no love, and sets himself up to judge his fellow Christians, grumbling about them and complaining about having to live in the same church with them, he merely shows his true colors. He falls short of the commandment Christ gave us and the example he set us; in this way, he himself sets the standard by which the Lord will judge him, when he comes.

This does not mean that we still have plenty of time in which to change for the better. The obligation to love others is something which cannot be postponed. In this connection, too, we must take the warning to heart: The Judge is already at the door. In what state will he find us, if he takes us completely by surprise? What are we personally prepared to do, so that our patient and all-conquering love for our brothers may enable our fellow Christians to spend their lives in the joyful expectation of the Lord's coming?

God Will Provide a Happy Ending (5:10–11)

Follow the Example of the Prophets (5 : 10)

¹⁰*Brothers, take the Prophets who spoke in the Lord's name as an example of suffering and patient endurance.*

The Christian who is called to give proof of his faith in an unbelieving world is not alone. His whole ancestry shows him that giving proof of one's faith in suffering and adversities is part of the Christian life. The great men we read of in the history of God's people set us an example to follow in our own lives. Not only do they show it is possible to hold out courageously to the last; they also reveal the magnificent reward this brings. The glory and the importance they enjoy among God's people are an indication of this. They constitute an appeal to Christians to follow their example, to join their company.

Another reason why St. James refers to the great men of the Old Testament is to remind us that we are their true followers and heirs. Like them, we too must bear witness for God and his Messiah. The prophets made God known to a faithless generation which looked askance at their message concerning him. In this verse, St. James consciously takes up Jesus' preaching. His own fellow countrymen were the heirs of those who had no love for the messengers God sent. They had even gone

so far as to persecute and silence them, because of the unwelcome message they preached. St. James includes among their
number all those who bore witness before their own people by
their obedience to God's word, from Abraham to the martyrs in
the days of the Maccabees. By the fate they suffered, this " cloud
of witnesses " (Heb. 12:1) prefigured and bore antecedent testimony to the " primordial witness " to the faith, our Lord Jesus
Christ who was crucified and raised to glory (cf. Heb. 12:1ff.).
St. James does not need to mention Jesus expressly. Every martyr
is a living witness to the Lord who suffered and triumphed
victoriously over evil.

Such witness is demanded of all those who belong to Christ
and are determined to prove themselves in this faith. It is only
such proof which really makes a believer a full member of God's
true people. Being a Christian, therefore, means joining company with those who have proved themselves, loyally and steadfastly, in the struggle for the faith, notwithstanding all that this
demands. It means bearing witness to Christ in this world by
means of one's own life.

It is Well for the Man Who Perseveres (5:11)

*11See how we say it is well for those who have persevered stead-
fastly. You have heard of Job's steadfastness, and you have before
your eyes the outcome God arranged for him, because God is
compassionate and merciful.*

It is true that we are incapable of bearing such witness by our
own efforts. But that is no excuse for giving up in despair.
On the contrary, we must look to the strength God gives; he

can inspire heroic courage and loyalty in weak human beings, and we must trust his gentle guidance. This is true especially when we are called to prove ourselves. God will always provide a happy ending. The call he makes is inspired by love and the hand he offers us introduces us into the sanctuary of his mercy. His love is determined to make us the gift of a share in his kingdom, in eternal happiness. The man who trusts God and entrusts himself to him will feel, in the midst of his difficulties, how wonderfully God guides his path, arranges his destiny, and grants him victory, even here and now.

This truth is beautifully illustrated by the story of Job, when his faith was put to the test. Not only was he granted the privilege of an immediate encounter with God, but he was also rewarded twice over for all that he had lost. God rewards those who have stood the test in this life as well as in the next; there is no limit to his graciousness. Even in the Old Testament people were familiar with the truth of faith expressed in the words: " God is merciful and compassionate " (Ps. 102 [103]: 8; 111 [112] : 4). St. James goes even further; God is full of mercy and compassion. This is demonstrated especially when a Christian is called to give proof of his faith. Such proof gives rise to steadfastness, and steadfastness brings a person's faith to perfection. This is the fruit of perfect faith, to which the reward of eternal happiness in union with God is promised. Consequently, we should be glad when God's love calls on us to stand the test. It is well for those who have persevered steadfastly.

THE CLOSING OF THE LETTER
(5:12-20)

CONCLUSION (5:12-20)

In this concluding section, St. James puts together a number of exhortations which are important for Christian life in the world; it seems there is no other connection between them. He speaks of swearing (5:12), of prayer (5:13–18), and of the care of Christians who were erring or had strayed (5:19). In this passage, his practical Christianity is once more demonstrated in all its basic power and realism. It gets its driving force from the power of prayer; it develops in an unsullied life of childlike trust and joy inspired by faith; and it finds its principal task in loving care for one's brother and his salvation. The fact that his letter ends with an appeal to care for those who have gone astray is not a sign of literary ineptitude on St. James's part. On the contrary, this appeal marks a return to the point with which he began in chapter 1, his anxiety that Christians who are tempted should stand the test successfully. At the same time, he once more expounds the basic principle of Christianity as it appeared to him and as he practiced it in his own life. The Christianity which consists in a lived faith which is put into practice is not something secondary; it is original, apostolic Christianity. Behind St. James's words we can hear his Lord and Master whose true witness and servant St. James is in every sentence of his letter. Therefore, anyone who listens to St. James hears our Lord Jesus Christ himself.

Above All, Do Not Take an Oath (5:12)

12Above all, my brothers, do not take an oath, neither by heaven nor by earth nor in any other form. Rather, let your Yes be Yes and your No be No, so that you will not incur judgment.

The deplorable habit of calling on God to witness the truth even of the banal and trivial affairs of everyday was widespread in Jewish and Jewish-Christian circles. In appearance, of course, people were scrupulous in observing the second commandment; they avoided using God's name and used various circumlocutions such as " Heaven," " Earth," or " The Temple " instead (cf. Mt. 5 : 33–37). Ultimately, however, all these expressions referred to God, so that he was dragged down to the level of everyday speech in this way. Moreover, the scribes arranged these circumlocutions very precisely according to their binding force. As a result, anyone who was familiar with their subtleties could outwit his fellow Christians by adapting a formula which had only an appearance of validity, and this often happened (cf. Mt. 23 : 16–22). Jesus had attacked this perversion of the truth and the shameful abuse of God's holiness it involved. He forbad his disciples to take an oath (Mt. 5 : 33–37). They were to avoid having to take an oath in any circumstances. As children of the same Father in heaven, their speech was to be direct, open, and truthful. Your Yes should be a simple Yes, and your No a simple No.

A follower of Christ must never resort to subtleties or half-truths; he must never indulge in sly schemes to defraud others, and he must avoid flattery and hypocrisy. He is called by God to speak the truth at all times and in all places. No matter where he goes, God's eyes are on him, and God champions the truth and passes judgment on all untruthfulness. A Christian is a disciple of that Lord and Master who lived and died as a witness to the truth. " He bore his witness in the presence of Pontius Pilate with his solemn Yes " (1 Tim. 6 : 13).

In this passage St. James, like Christ himself, has no intention of laying down a general law for the whole world. Therefore, he does not mean to oblige Christians to refuse to take an oath, when it is justifiably demanded of them, to discover the truth. On the contrary, he wants to impress upon Christians that they are bound to speak the truth at all times and in all places; they must renounce all insincerity and trickery, and refuse to abuse God's sacred authority for their own purposes or according to their own whims. The man who has been rescued from the prince of this world, the father of lies, must live the truth, both in his words and in his conduct. It is only in this way that the world can be brought to salvation and the church made holy. A Christian is bound to live the truth in love (cf. 4:15). Then truth will penetrate a world which is governed by lying and hypocrisy, by confusion and distrust, by guile and deceit. It depends upon us whether God's saving spirit of truth will penetrate our surroundings, our communities, and the world at large, and bring them healing. That is why, if a man fails in this respect, he should not be surprised when God calls him to account for it. God champions the truth and he watches over all we say and do.

Pray in All the Circumstances of Your Lives (5:13–18)

In Joy and Sorrow (5:13)

¹³*Is any one of you forced to endure suffering? He should pray. Is anyone happy? Let him sing a song of praise.*

The strength to endure suffering properly is to be found in prayer, in a union of trust with God. It is in virtue of this union that a Christian will be able to accept and endure all that God's will sends his children or allows to happen to them. We are not left to our own resources; we are not condemned to silence when we are put to the test. On the contrary, God has given us a tongue; he has poured out his love in our hearts. He listens to his children when they appeal to him, and he helps them to endure their sufferings and distress victoriously. However, man must call upon God; that is his part, the gift which has been given him and the strength he enjoys. Consequently, the only genuine faith is one which is rooted in prayer. A faith which is professed only as an intellectual conviction can never enable a person to endure suffering.

Prayer, however, is much more than a means of obtaining help in need; it is the immediate expression of a living faith. It is in prayer that faith lives and acts; in prayer that it takes flesh and visible form. It is prayer that reveals the living power of faith. Having faith, therefore, means praying, living by, with and in God, in a mutual exchange of love.

Prayer encompasses all the circumstances of life. This is what St. James wants to indicate by his choice of the contrary terms joy and sorrow. Praising God is as much a part of prayer as petition or thanksgiving. Such praise gladly makes use of the songs and prayers of sacred scripture, the psalms (The Greek term *psallein* which St. James uses here clearly alludes to this). In God's eyes, the Christian who appears before him is a member of a people. Consequently, a Christian makes use of the songs of the Old Testament people of God to offer him his petitions, his praise, and his thanks. His personal prayer is taken up into the choir of God's people, before and after Christ. This people of God is still on the way to his kingdom, the goal of all the long course of saving history. The fact that its prayer is subject to this divine disposition holds good for the Christians of all ages.

In Sickness and in Sin (5:14–18)

[14]*Is one of you ill? He should call the presbyters in the community to him, and they must pray over him and anoint him with oil in the name of the Lord.* [15]*Such prayer, inspired by faith, will heal the sick person, and the Lord will raise him up, and if he has committed sins, they will be forgiven him.*

St. James recognizes a particularly efficacious form of prayer which is offered by the church for those who are ill, the sacrament of the sick. He is clearly referring to a usage practiced by the church which is taken for granted. Those responsible for the pastoral care of the community (who are here called presbyters—elders—although young men such as Timothy were also found among them) enjoyed a special sacramental power. The prayer they offered for the sick person, accompanied by a rite in which his body was anointed with olive oil and the name of Jesus was invoked, had special powers of healing. It overcame the patient's illness and helped him to leave his bed and get about. Many illnesses are the result of a person's own sins. Jesus forgives these, when the presbyters pronounce their sacramentally effective prayer in his name over their fellow Christian who is ill. Therefore, it is the Lord himself who is at work in this sacrament, by means of those who hold the office of presbyter; it is he who cures and forgives; it is he who raises up the sick person and saves him. In the same way, the church pronounces this sacramental prayer for the sick in his name, that is, by his authority.

Of course, it is true in this instance as in all others that a Christian must commit his prayer to the Lord and through him to God the Father; " thy will be done." The sacrament does not produce its effect magically; it is not just an efficient mechanism. Its effect is determined by a person; God decides what is good for the sick man who may often be suffering as the result of his own sins. However, this does not entitle us to disregard this saving gift by using it only as a last resort, when death is imminent. We must trust God; in every serious illness we must enter into this lifegiving communion with Jesus which can bring us to salvation. Obviously, it is a wonderful gift that God should have such care for our bodily lives. In his love, he takes charge of our illnesses, and endows his priests with special gifts to help Christians who are ill.

This does not exclude the use of those means of healing which man himself has at his disposal. It is God who has given man these means and these possibilities, and he means them to be used. Yet, it is only by referring to Christ that we can see the real meaning of sickness and how sin, its hidden root, can be cured. If we are united with him, we can see that illness is meant to purify us, and that if it is his will we shall regain our physical health, as a result of our trust in him. These are gifts which can only come from our Saviour Jesus Christ. As well as introducing us into a deeper communion with Christ, illness can also bring us into communion with the church. This grace is granted us by Christ's ministers. Every illness helps to further the progress of the church. Illness enriches us, if we endure it in a spirit of faith, as members of the church. And the church is enriched when its members bring even their illnesses and their sins to it in a spirit of faith and so move the Lord to act.

16Confess your sins to one another, therefore, and pray for each other, so that you may be healed. The efficacious prayer of a just man can accomplish many things. [17]*Elias was a human being like ourselves, and when he prayed earnestly that rain would not come, no rain fell on the earth for three years and six months.* [18]*And when he prayed once more, heaven yielded its rain and the earth brought forth its fruit.*

St. James here introduces a new idea concerning our attitude towards our fellow Christians, and draws attention to a fresh aspect of the prayer offered by the church. This is intercessory prayer offered by Christians for one another, but especially for those who are in need. These verses contain an appeal to all Christians to pray for one another, but especially for those who are ill, that God may grant them healing without delay. God is not content merely to introduce the Christian who is ill more deeply into his community, the church; at one and the same time he also reminds the community of its obligation to pray for the sick. A Christian's prayer is all-powerful, when it is disinterested and offered in the right spirit. There is no limit to the blessings which are showered upon the world because of the intercessory prayers offered by Christians; harm is averted, evil is turned to good, and what is good already is brought to perfection. The fate of the world depends to a large extent on the prayers offered by good people, on their intercession in the name of humanity.

Striking examples of this are to be found in the Old Testament. St. James mentions the prayer offered by the prophet Elias; it was capable even of altering the course of the seasons. And yet the fact remains that he was a human being just like us.

Such prayer, however, must be inspired by a love of one's brother which is sincere and disinterested. The confession of sins which takes place at the beginning of the liturgy must rid us above all of all faults against fraternal charity. Genuine prayer can come only from a heart which has been purified. Jesus expressly demands that we should be reconciled with our brother and forgive those who are indebted to us, before we come to pray (cf. Mt. 5:23–26; 18:23–35). That is why the early church began the liturgical service with a prayer offered in common for the forgiveness of sins. The *Confiteor* which we say before Mass nowadays corresponds to this ancient rite; it arose from this public avowal of sins. Its purpose is to put an end to discord and ensure that those who are about to pray will be pleasing to God and just in his eyes. It is only then that their prayer will be heard.

However, their prayer must be made in earnest. This is the force of the word " efficacious." It must be made with the full power of an undivided faith; it must be persevering in its plea for a fellow Christian and his salvation, and it must be prompted by unselfish love.

Prayer such as this is capable of great things, even though the person who offers it is only a poor, weak human being. It can avert evil and insure the well-being and the salvation of a fellow Christian. Like the prayer Elias offered, it can even lead the world to God and to salvation. Here once again, St. James echoes faithfully the teaching of his Lord who demanded a faith which could move mountains (Mt. 17:20). This gives us some idea of the importance of the intercessory prayer offered by the church for the salvation of its members and of the whole world. It is clearly a wonderful favor to know that we enjoy the protection of the church's prayer. This should certainly impel all of us to take our place in this chain of intercession, and so make our contribution to the healing and the salvation of all baptized Christians and of the whole human race. However, it should also move us to examine our consciences; have we really got our brother's interests at heart, together with those of our fellow men, and the salvation of the whole world? It may be that our selfishness and lack of love sap the strength of our faith, so that our prayer is unavailing.

Have a Care for Your Brother who Has Strayed (5:19-20)

¹⁹My brothers, if one of your number has strayed from the truth and someone brings him to repentance, ²⁰you can be sure that: The man who has saved a sinner from the wrong path and brought him to repentance, saves his soul from death and "covers a multitude of sins" (Prov. 10:12).

A Christian is responsible for his fellow Christians who share the same faith with him; he is doubly so, if his fellow Christian has abandoned the faith and is in danger of being lost eternally. We cannot be indifferent to the fate which threatens the "lost sheep" of the church. A real Christian must not be so overjoyed at the thought of his own salvation that he exhausts all his efforts in making sure of it. The Lord's love for those who are lost must inspire us to go after our lost brother and bring him to repentance. This sentence closes the section devoted to the intercessory prayer offered by Christians. Prayer is the principal means we must use in our striving to find our brother who has strayed. And it is an efficacious means. St. James realizes that it is not easy to bring a person who has gone astray and is threatened with damnation to repentance. That is why we must have recourse to this powerful means of salvation, prayer of intercession; we must give ourselves to it perseveringly and in a spirit of faith, until the Lord grants our request and the Christian who has been lost is found. On the other hand, we must not forget what a joy it is when life is restored to a man who had become the prey of death, when a Christian who has been lost is found. The Lord himself gave us a striking picture of this unbounded joy in his parables about those who were lost (Lk. 15). There is joy then, not merely on earth, among the brothers of the Christian who has been found again, but also in heaven. This is joy such as existed in heaven and in the church when I, too, was found by God, through Jesus Christ.

The repentant sinner will himself be the greatest reward his rescuer will enjoy; his salvation means that he will be united with him for ever in a lifegiving communion in God's kingdom. Moreover, God will also reward him in overflowing measure for his active love. Such "love covers a multitude of sins," as St. James tells us in this verse. The man who saves his brother saves himself. Love such as his wipes out all his own sins.

St. James's letter, therefore, returns once more to its starting-point, his anxiety for the salvation of Christians who are being tempted. He is determined to bring to salvation all those who are called to it. And how? By calling upon them to take their faith seriously, to live as Christians who practice what they profess. Time is short; the Lord is coming. Only a practical faith can bring a Christian and his brothers, and the whole world as well, to salvation. The holiness St. James preaches is not something based on deeds alone; the Lord's brother and his servant, he is well aware that only the man who does God's will belongs to Christ. Only to such a man has the promise of salvation been made. St. James's letter, therefore, constitutes an appeal to us to take our faith seriously, and to live it, in deed and in truth; cannot afford to turn a deaf ear to his call.